State Actors Vs. Not State Actors

Volume 2: The Not State Actors

Paolo Dealberti

Forward

Rev. Shigenobu Watanabe

Hongwanji Buddhist Mission of Australia

1. Edition 2012

2. Edition 2015

ISBN-13: 978-1514756836
ISBN-10: 1514756838

Verkauft durch JEWIR- Deutschland

To my Mother

What was forecast in Prosumerzen and Westphalia XXI at least one year before?

1. **The dangerously oversized myth of the global middleclass**: the global economic slowdown and the rising of organized movements of protests plus the general lack of legitimacy of the leaderships are been confirming what wrote more than one year ago
2. **Turkey will be not pro-Iran and Islamist,(at least for now)**:the Turkish aptitude toward the Egyptian situation and the war between Israel and Gaza - November 2012 – are evidences that confirms what we wrote more than one year ago when the overwhelming majority of analysts were concer5ned about an "Islamic and pro-Iran" Turkey
3. **Germany ´s unsustainable growth**: The slowdown inside the Germany economy in 2012 and the forecast for 2013-14 are the confirm of what wrote at least 1 year before and when the great majority of analysts were able only to talk about "Super & Invincible Deutschland". An additional confirm is published one year later:: Adam Tooze, Germany´s unsustainable growth ,Foreign Affairs Volume 91 N. 5 Sept./Oct. 2012)
4. **A nuclear Iran could be a stabilizing factor**: more than one year later a confirm inside Kenneth N. Waltz "Why Iran should get the bomb". Foreign Affairs Vol. 91 N.4 Jul(Aug 2012
5. **The Italian political crisis**: one year later both the Administrative Elections and the Election in Sicily confirmed what we have told
6. **The nazi killer is not crazy**: the sentence one year later confirmed the background of connections

accusing the same entities we have mentioned and that the assassin was neither crazy nor alone

7. **The BRIC's are more a "paper tiger" than a real global power:** more than one year later the prestigious Foreign Affairs confirmed this vision in Ruchir Sharma – The Demise of the Rest –FA Vol.91/6 Nov-Dec 2012

8. **The Christian fundamentalism is a problem:** after one year what wrote in our articles was confirmed by a Foreign Policy 's prestigious panel of the top 72 worldwide thinkers about strategy that classified the Christian fundamentalism as the 3rd biggest and dangerous menace foe the USA

9. **Al Qaeda is a yesterday's terrorism problem:** after one year what wrote in our articles was confirmed by a Foreign Policy 's prestigious panel of the top 72 worldwide thinkers about strategy

10. **The Pentagon bloat:** : after one year what wrote in our articles was confirmed by a Foreign Policy 's prestigious panel of the top 72 worldwide thinkers about strategy

This world is **complex and not complicate**. Unlucky an incompetent worldwide leadership is not able to understand the difference between complex and complicate.

And we can forget that they can handle that...

Index

3) The Not State Actors (Volume 2)

----

1) The Global   Scenario (Volume 1)

C.1:Humpolitics

C2:The questions behind the real balance of power

C.3 The 28 different forms of Non State Actors

C.4:Happiness as geo-politic key-factor!

C.5: World middle-class: how a self-fuelling "myth" could be used by someone to affect our democracies (I)

C.6:TACTICAL WARNING: WAR 2012 (AS PROSUMERZEN IS TELLING SINCE EVER)

2)The State Actors

C.7: Obama, 15-06-2011 and the 9 nations of the USA p

C.8: Turkey a skilled broker … (1/2) (II)

C.9: Turkey a skilled broker (2/2) (III)

C.10: Germany, France, the UK and the EU…who needs whom?

C.11:Greece and the EU (or EEC + €), (1/2) (IV)

C.12:Greece and the EU (or EEC + €), (2/2) (V)

C.13Chancellor Merkel & Co.: crisis of legitimacy (VI)

C.14: Israel and Iran: the Indo-Pakistani model (or Iran will generate a Sunni Muslim Holocaust) (VII)

C.15: Jasmine Revolution: Israel and Palestine: Nuclear Iran vs. Nuclear Israel (VIII)

C.17: Iran? Al Qaeda?

C.18: Post Scriptum: Iran? Al Qaeda?

C.19: The BIIIIIIIIIIIIIG cut: the US deficit (IX)

C.20: Arrogant Capitals: New York and Washington…(Arrogant for the USA)

C.21: B &B, the two losers in Italy (X)

C.22: Pakistan and the Kingdom of Saudi Arabia, (The Islamabad Card)

C.23: Dong Feng (Superpower China)

C.24:2 Libyas …

C.25: Libya: at least 8 Lessons

C.26: Germany and the EU: who needs whom?
p.136 (X)

C.27: The Shoah in a not neo nazi Germany

C.28:Neo-nazi Germany? Not at all

(I) (Editorial Note: The global economic slowdown and the rising of organized movements of protests plus the general lack of legitimacy of the leaderships are been confirming what wrote more than one year ago)

(II),(III),(Editorial Note: The Turkish aptitude toward the Egyptian situation and the war between Israel and Gaza - November 2012 – are evidences that confirms what we wrote more than one year ago when the overwhelming majority of analysts were concer5ned about an "Islamic and pro-Iran" Turkey)

(III),(IV),(V),(VI),(X), (Editorial Note: The slowdown inside the Germany economy in 2012 and the forecast for 2014 are the confirm of what wrote at least 1 year before and when the great majority of analysts were able only to talk about "Super & Invincible Deutschland". An additional confirm is published one year later:: Adam Tooze, Germany´s unsustainable growth ,Foreign Affairs Volume 91 N. 5 Sept./Oct. 2012)

(VII),(VIII) (Editorial note: more than one year later a confirm inside Kenneth N. Waltz "Why Iran should get the bomb". Foreign Affairs Vol. 91 N.4 Jul(Aug 2012)

(IX)(Editorial note: the Pentagon bloat was confirmed one year later by a Foreign Policy s panel composed by the 72 of the most brilliant analysts in the world.

(X) (Editorial Note: one year later both the Administrative Elections and the Election in Sicily confirmed what we have told)

(XI)The sentence one year later confirmed the background of connections accusing the same entities we have mentioned and that the assassin was neither crazy nor alone)

(XII),(XIII),(XIV)(Editorial Note: more than one year later the prestigious Foreign Affairs confirmed this vision in Ruchir Sharma – The Demise of the Rest –FA Vol.91/6 Nov-Dec 2012)

Foreword

Human Love and The Love of the Buddha

Paolo Dealberti is challenging the common wisdom calling our critical spirits to follow him in a new dimension of geopolitics. A sort of terra incognita called Humpolitics.

*A geopolitics that is human and that can be described,(with a new word he invented), as "**Humpolitics**" = human+politics".*

In his book, Paolo Dealberti, places the human beings at the center of geo-politics, geo-finance and geo-economy and ethic as the practical tool to achieve a global level of happiness.

Dealberti´s approach is not theoretical but laser focused on examples analyzed under a multi-disciplinary approach.

Extremely important is the description of the State Actors,(SA´s), that are the real players inside the world arena. A description that finds its confirm inside the accuracy of the innovative description of the 28 forms of Non State Actors, (NSA´s).

A description that is not only theory but that finds 17 examples of forms of Non State Actors inside the books to be explained and among them the most interesting are these about the historical background of the recent form of NSA´s ,(originated in the XVII),and about how they act and interact inside the financial crisis since 2008.

Paolo Dealberti, page after page ,is collecting each kaleidoscopic element and draws the whole picture of a world that once was complicate and that today is evolving into complexity. Dealberti is able to find new key words able to explain this dynamic complexity because our traditional partitions, (North & South, left & right, progressive & conservative, industrial & financial economy…), simply belong to the past. A past that started long time ago if, for example, we think that the first to talk about a multi-polar post cold war was President Nixon…and it was 1972!

Ethic is a form of love and love can have different form.

Concerning compassion, there is a difference between the Path of Sages and the Pure Land Path. Compassion in the Path of Sages is to pity, commiserate with, and care for beings. It is extremely difficult, however, to accomplish the saving of others just as one wishes.

Compassion in the Pure Land Path should be understood as first attaining Buddhahood quickly through saying the nembutsu and, with the mind of great love and great compassion, freely benefiting sentient beings as one wishes.

However much love and pity we may feel in our present lives, it is hard to save others as we wish; hence, such compassion remains unfulfilled. Only the saying of the nembutsu, then, is the mind of great compassion that is thoroughgoing. Thus were his words.

(Tannisho - Chapter 4 -)

First of all, I would like to share a conversation between a King and a Queen, which is in one of the Sutras called "Sho-man-Kyo".

- One day, the Kind asked the Queen,

"How much do you love me?"

A little later, Queen replied,

"I never ever loved any other person other than myself."

Then, the King thought for a while and said,

"Oh, dear Queen, I am so grateful that you love me that much!" -

This conversation is a bit puzzling for ordinary people. It is like a Zen question called "Ko-an"(e.g.1).

However, it tells us a true part of human being's feelings. The Queen said that her most important object to love is herself, nobody else. She was confessing opening her mind widely to the King, her husband. The King also understood the Queen, his beloved wife, had disclosed her true mind to him. That's why her words caught the King's attention.

Human love is always incomplete, because of the self-centered nature of human being, while Amida Buddha's compassion/love is absolutely unconditional. Shinran Shonin describes the difference between human love and the Buddha's compassion/love in terms of the difference between the "Path of the Sages „and the "Path of the Pure Land." A sage may pity, sympathies with, or care for other human beings. But, sooner or later, he will reach the limit of his love for others. He will always have the tendency to love himself the most. Therefore, his love is not something that truly endures. From his writings, it is clear that Shinran Shonin thought deeply about love and compassion, and that he tried sincerely to love others, even when they broke his heart. Yet, he yearned for the unconditional love that characterized Amida Buddha's compassion.

He said:

"However much love and pity we may feel in our present lives, it is hard to save others as we wish; hence, such

compassion remains unfulfilled. Only the saying of the nembutsu, then, is the mind of great compassion that is thoroughgoing."("Tannisho" - Chapter 4 -)

Therefore, Shinran Shonin discovered that unconditional, pure love can only be found in the mind of Amida Buddha. Traditionally, there are three levels of love described in the Buddhist teaching.

These are;

1. Conditional Love :This is a type of love that exists between human beings. It is instinctive, temporary and conditional, varying with the time, place and the particular people involved.

2. Rational Love: This is the love that arises from the philosophical understanding that all being are equal, and is a purely rational sort of love.

3. Unconditional Love: This is the pure love that can arise only in the absence of ego. In traditional love, there is no consideration given to time or place, person or means. This is the dynamic love of Amida Buddha, which is for everyone.

The Lager Sutra says, "The Buddha mind is great compassion and mercy. It brings everyone to the Pure Land through unconditional love."

Tenjin Bosatsu (Vasbandhu) also wrote that, "Amida's love is all-encompassing, just like earth, water, fire, wind and air."

*Donran Daishi (T'an
Luan) explains Ryuju Bisatsu(Nagarjuna)'s simile as follows:*

"Earth holds everything in itself; water enters planets regardless of whether they are poisonous or beneficial; fire

burns anything, regardless of whether it has a pleasant or un offensive smell; wind blows on anyone, regardless or whether or not he is awake; air fills all space equally without distinction. In the same way, the Buddha' love leaves nothing untouched or excluded."

After a person has heard of the unlimited compassion granted to everyone through Amida's Universal Vow, he becomes able to regard all beings with friendliness and brotherly love.

As T'an Luan wrote,

"We are brothers and sisters all over the world."

Again, as Shinran Shonin said,

"For all sentient beings, without exception, have been our parents and brothers and sisters in the course of countless lives in many states of existence." "Tannisho" - Chapter 5 - .

Dealberti´s vision of the world is a realistic one where all the players, Public Governments /SA´s as well as Private Governments/NSA´s, leave not man behind in order to create a sustainable future...because "We are brothers and sisters all over the world."

Rev. Shigenobu Watanabe

Hongwanji Buddhist Mission of Australia

Introduction

It is a war between the Post Westphalia Order and the Evolution of the Post Westphalia Order,("Westphalia XXI").

This world needs new rules for old players as well as old rules for new players.

Old? New?

Words that are more meaningless than we are used to think and accept because the only tradition that lasts is that all change ... within tradition.

We are what we see and we see according to what we belong to. Then we are used believe that this is objectivity and ,if we are fundamentalists, that this is the only way,

 Reality is how we see the world and not how is made of ...!

Our contemporary world is not born in 1989,(the end of the USSR),1968,(Internet),1945,(Yalta and Breton Woods), and we "simply" will not change it thanks to our social newtorks

Its last great transformation was made in 1648 with the Peace of Westphalia. An event deep rooted within the tradition of structures that were born centuries before.

Fernand Braudel and Jacques Attali, among others, are telling us that our present belongs to an old,(really old),past.

Starting from that we have created a network of Internet Magazines now integrated inside one of the few an Integrated Cross-media Platform,(*).The articles in this book were published in 2011 and 2012 in Prosumerzen and in Westphalia XXI,(NOTE: today, 2015,both are replaced by AppealPower www.appealpower.com)

They talk about a… war.

A war between old powers, (that are not so old),and new ones,(that are not so new).

The protagonists of this war are the State Actors, (SA´s), and the Non State Actors, (NSA´s). **Or, better, the Public Governments vs. the Private Governments.**

In the first section of this book, (The Global Scenario), I describe the global scenario classifying the most important State Actors in the world inside the 38 exchequers of the planet:

- **The Global player:** The USA

- **The Supra- regional influential powers**: The P.R. of China, France, Japan, the UK
- **The Regional influential players**: Brasil, Germany, the KSA, India, Iran, Israel, Russia, Turkey
- **Local Influential Players:**
  Algeria,Angola,Argentina,Australia,Azerbijan,Banglad esh,Canada,CH,Colombia,Cuba,DominicanRep.,Egyp t,Greece,Holland,Indonesia,Ireland,Italy,Kazakhstan, Kenya,Latvia,Niger,Nigeria,Pakistan,Panama,Poland, R.D. of Congo , S. Korea, Senegal, Serbia, Somalia, South Africa, Sweden, Syria, UAE, Ukraine, Venezuela, Vietnam

Then I described the **28 forms of Non State Actors**. Usually they are described with five but their complexity requires a more detailed and deeper evaluation.

The last part of the 1st section is dedicated to the values of an human based geo-politics,(Humpolitics),importance of the "Gross Happiness Index" and **about the risk for the democracy of a self-generated myth of a world-class middle class.**

The second part,(State Actors),is dedicated to most important State Actors in the last year:

China, France, Germany, Greece, India, Iran, Israel , Italy, Libya, Pakistan, Palestine, The KSA, The UK, The US, Turkey, Venezuela

The third section is dedicated to the Non State Actors offering real examples and evidences about the classification in 28 forms in the first section.

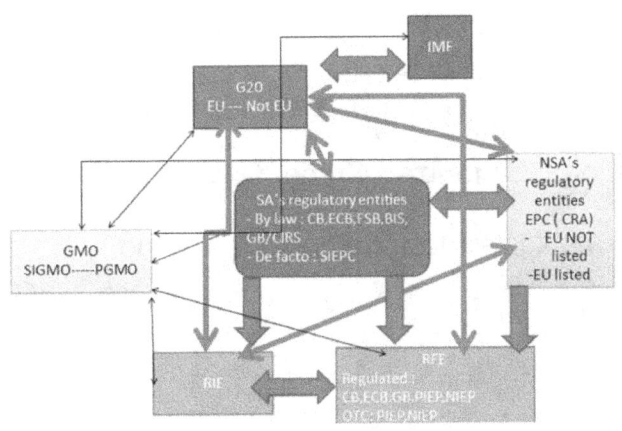

(Interactions between the Real Industrial Economy, the Real Financial Economy inside the financial and economic crisis since 2008 - ©2012 all rights reserved Paolo Dealberti)

It is possible to find the follow examples of forms of Not State Actors:

1. Private Financial Controllers: C.29,30,31,32,35,36,37

2. International Organizations:C.44

3. Regional Organizations: C.29,30,31,32,35,37

4. Functional Organizations:

    C.29,30,31,32,35,37,44,48,49

5. Supervising International Organizations :

    C 29,30,31,32,35,37,38

6. Transnational Organized Crime: C 37,42,43,56

7. Multinationals like State Actors,(Power Inc.) :
    C.33,34,41

8. NGO:C.41

9. Private Security Forces/Contractors: C. 33,34,41

10. State Actors within Failed States: C 34

11. Holistic Powers: C.39,46

12. Global Media Outlet:C.29,30,31,32,39

13. International Consulting Company: C.40

14. Private International Powerhouses:

   C.29,30,31,32,33,35,36,38

15. Terrorism:C.C.45

16. Global Diaspora:C.54,55,57

17. Nation Within Stares:C.58

If it would be possible to travel into the past we will discover that nothing is new under the sun but at the same time we will learn that a lot of new "things" are still waiting for being described und understood.

In front of us we have an almost blank page and it is upon to us chose the future we want.

Each of us can write the future and this according to our culture and social environment because history never ends.

Paolo Dealberti, Munich 23-11-2012

The
Not State
Actors

(Private
Governments)

(Form of NSA: Private Financial Controllers, Functional Organizations,

Supervising International Organizations, Transnational Organized Crime,

Regional Organizations, Private International Powerhouse)

Chap 29 - The rating index: is the end of the SA´s soft power? (1/4)

Westphalia XXI, 28-6-2012

You can borrow till someone lends to you. That means that if you abuse of it ,(too much debt till to reach a situation of potential default),is simply because there was a lender irresponsible like you that lends to you money,(without any prudence in term of basic risk management), for his profit.

Greece, Germany, France and Italy do you remember?

Or in clear text:

-        Greece: the irresponsible borrower with political elected elite ,(PEE);that gained from it

-        France and Germany: the irresponsible lenders with the elites either of global systematically important banks and multinationals and their political supporters gained of it and for that their banks are at risk a lot more then these of other EU Countries[i]

-        Italy: the irresponsible borrower with a political elected elite that gained from it but among the gainers we have also to list the Germans banks interested on lending to Italy because Rome is the 5th world market,(just after the USA),for Germany and China is the 7th after Austria as well as we have to list the French ones because Italy is the 2nd world market   for Made in France and China is the 9th[ii].

On clear text the relation can be described as follow: if German and French banks buy Italian sovereigns that mean for the Berlin a bigger 5th world market and for the Paris a bigger 2nd one. But not only that because France is the 1st world market for Germany as well as Germany is the biggest market in the world for France and if Paris and Berlin can gain more exporting to Rome it is also clear that they become richer and one can export more to the other. At the end of the day both the irresponsible borrowers and the irresponsible lenders benefit from this situation.

And why both were irresponsible is now more than clear as it is clear that all kinds of elites,(political, industrial and financial), gained from it in each of the mentioned Countries.

Before that we go ahead we want to magnify that this is neither a Marxist-style analysis nor a no-global-anonymous-style one and this allows us to introduce other actors but before of that we have to explain how we consider them.

State Actors and Non State Actors and their relation of powers facing the public interests is the chessboard where we develop our analysis.

<u>Even if we do neither underestimate and not under evaluate</u> the Greece structural budget problems,(for example due to a poor tax collection or to a too generous retirement system), we want also to focus to an important but too often totally missed additional element of the debt crisis: **that of the debt holds by foreign banks and used by Greece to pay companies that come from the same countries.**

It is now clear that the problem started "not only as" direct consequence of the American mortgage crisis but ,(and "simply"), because it was reached the level where Greece cannot pay back the debts with France and Germany used to pay infrastructure built up by German and French multinationals. If you prefer with the right hand Athens borrowed by French and German banks the money used by the left hand to pay French and Germans multinationals involved to build up infrastructures in the country, (it is told that the Olympic Games were the *"mother of all debts"*).Infrastructures that generated jobs and wealth and with them also political consensus . Thank to this mechanism were possible to obtain *"the perfect quadrature of the circle "*here the financial, industrial and political elites in each country can benefit in term of revenues or of votes.
At that point instead to solve it as a controllable and local banks crisis the political leaderships in Berlin and in Paris wanted to drill it for opportunistic and populist electoral reasons. The ratio was to gain internal electoral consensus and also to impose their leadership in Europe. For Merkel and Sarkozy was easy to think that due to the intrinsic weakness of the Italian politic landscape and the Spanish

weakness as country vs. France and Germany. They were also sure that London will follows its own political trajectory,(and by the way London is internationally stronger than Berlin and Paris for a lot of soft as well as hard assets).The situation is not changed on June 2012 where :

I) in Italy after the local elections on May we have that all the national parties are de facto not national in the sense that they need to develop electoral tickets with he local new political forces,(Civic Lists), to be able to win and to win only inside a coalition. At the same time the landscape is so fragile that these local forces need to be allied with the "national" one in order to generate a ticket to be able to have a national voice, (by the way this is because Berlusconi wants to create a network of Civic Lists).

II) In Spain the government is fragile

Till now for both President Sarkozy and for Chancellor Markel this decision is not been generating any electoral success. They lost an election after the other since the beginning of the crisis and Sarkozy lost the Presidency.

And at European level it is also not so clear their leadership also because Berlin and Paris have not the money to "lead the dance". But not only this because Germany and France cannot afford to leave the EU if for example, Germany generated 80% of the gins for export in the Union and China is only its 5h market ,(Italy is the 6th),and not other BRICS is in the top 10 world markets,(this according to D-Statistis 2012 for the year 2011). Paris and Berlin cannot "say no " to the EU and if they leave the euro with currencies ,(mark and franc), with a 20%-30% higher value than the European currency it will be for them a problem to export even in Belgium or Italy but not for Brussels and Rome to export to them with a 20%-30% cheaper currency,(euro). It is also logic that we can expect some kind or reduced growth in France and in Germany when the 2nd biggest world market of the first and the 6ht of the latter are in deep recession. By the way we are talking about a EU Country like Italy.

Or, better, Standard & poor's and Moody's could do more than Chancellor Merkel and President Sarkozy, (and today more than Chancellor Merkel and President Hollande),to convince worldwide investors to buy or not to buy the sovereigns of EU Countries in crisis.

And Chancellor Merkel cannot do a lot ,(and surely lees then we are used to credit), if Commerzbank have problems to find a buyer for its share in a top Russian bank and without that money Moody's will not improve the rating. Or she can also do nothing if the Landsbank of Bayern , a Land controlled by the sister party CSU, since 2008 has accumulated a growing deficit of ten billions euros. Maybe the day that Berlin has to pay this bill the Chancellor will re-consider her approach about the euro-bond and she will ask to all to pay for it. Something not new for Berlin if we consider what happened in the late spring 2011 when Germany accused Spain to be the origin of the e-coli bacteria and ruined its export. The consequence was that the whole EU paid to Spain more than 200 million € as indemnification. We repeat the whole EU and not only Berlin that generated this problem and, of course, that day was more than normal for the Chancellor to *"ask to share the burden"* of the cost for a problem generated only by her government and its false accuses. Or it was not *"against a wise budgetary policy"* when in January 2012 the new Italian Government reduced the fine for tax evasion to a leading Germany multinational from 1.5 billion € to only 300 million € ,(and doing that avoided the bankruptcy of the multinational that told that had not the money to pay it) . That time to condone a German tax evader was considered *"moral and European"* by a Chancellor always ready to teach about ethic, virtuous and moral management of public finances that must have a "zero tolerance" against tax evaders.

In other term the stronger elites of the stronger EU Countries **suffer a dramatic lack of credibility and popularity**. And not mention about these of other countries in Europe like Italy, Greece or Portugal.
Inside this frame the Rating Agencies simply fulfilled a vacuum of powers generated by this lack of credibility.
In other terms: they are strong because others, (the political powers), are weaks

Notes

---

[i] European Banking Authority 2011 EU-wide stress test aggregate report http://stress-test.eba.europa.eu/pdf/EBA_ST_2011_Summary_Report_v6 .pdf

[ii] Institut national de la Statistique et des Etudes economiques ,2011www.insee.fr

Statisches Bundesamt Deutschland ,2011 www.destatis.de

(Private Financial Controllers,Functional Organizations,Supervising

International Organizations,Transnational Organized Crime,Regional

Organizations,Private International Powerhouse)

Chap.30 -The rating index: is the end of the SA´s soft

power? (2/4)

Westphalia XXI 29-6-2012

1- When? *The historical background*

As usual Foreign Affairs has the pulse of the world and it is not by coincidence that his last issue[i] is titled "the clash of ideas". Before of that the world in a 48 years long period, (from 1962 to 2010), was described as:

- The place of the global village[ii]^,1962
- The place where new influential minorities are the strategic elites in modern society and beyond the ruling class[iii],1963
- The place that will face the shock of the future[iv],1970
- The place for the "Post-Cold War World[v]",1972
- The place where an overstretched superpower collapses[vi],1987
- The place for the end of history[vii],1989
- The place where who masters the soft power holds the strongest form of power[viii].,1990
- The place for hidden technocrats that represent a new class and a new capitalism[ix] ,1992
- The place for the "clash of civilizations"[x] ,1993

- The place of the post-capitalist society[xi],1994
- The place for the end of the nation state[xii],1995
- The place for the "clash of globalizations"[xiii] ,2002
- The place where the hyper-empire will clash with the hyper-democracy inside the last evolution of a globalization that started in the Flanders in the XIII [xiv],2006
- The place for the "clash of emotions"[xv] ,2007
- The place where the Jihad has lost and has not chance to run the world and where is growing the alternative model of authoritarian great powers like China or Russia[xvi],2007
- The place for a nonpolar order[xvii],2008
- The place of the "Zweite Moderne",
(2nd modernity")[xviii],2009
- The place where the West rules....at least for now[xix],2010
- The place of the post-Washington
Consensus[xx] where the solution seems to be more state,2011

In the second decade of the XXI the world is described as the place of the "clash of ideas" where we have always to keep in mind that ideas are perceptions that are the result of a mix between culture and emotions. And for Gideon Rose, (editor of FA), on 2012 that means to make modernity work with the reconciliation of capitalism and democracy[xxi].His editorial is a brilliant analysis that talks about a carefully selections of ideas that still shape the world and the modernity. Roses is in deep touch with the world when he points out the need of a reconciliation between capitalism and democracy and because the FA 's issue starts with Lenin we have to back to the XIX.

The deep meaning of it is that we can describe *"our time"* as an historical moment where:

-The political economy follows ideas of the XX

-The world order is facing the struggles of the last evolution of the Post Westphalia Order, (PWO), as originated in the XVII[xxii]
- The social science is based on rules of the XX

- The world structure of the financial markets is the last evolution of the *Fiera del Danaro in Piacenza,* (Italy.1579), where a super-elite of sixty world class bankers met to decide the trends inside the monetary world markets and of the first stock exchange in Amsterdam,(1622)[xxiii]
- The religions on centuries old belief even if we are assisting of the creation of a new world wide religion[xxiv]
-The soft-power is based on rules of the XX[xxv]
- The technology on XXI applications from smart phones, holographic brokers for "real time" consulting about the financial markets to Virtual Worlds

But it is also a world where we face political and territorial tensions that back to the Treaty of Versailles at the end of the 1st World War that lasted frozen during the Cold War and are still struggling,(if not exploding), in the second decade of the XXI.

A synthesis of this situation tells that we are living in a sort of **"temporal limbo"** where ideas, emotions and institutions born in the XII, XVII... XX, XXI take the forms of the clash of cultures, emotions and ideas that we are struggling.

Notes:

[i] Foreign Affairs Special Anniversary Issue , "The Clash of Ideas . The ideological Battles That Made the Modern World And Will Shape the Future" , Vol. 91 /N. 1 Jan.-Feb.2012
[ii] Marshall McLuhan." books The Gutenberg Galaxy: The Making of Typographic Man", 1962
[iii] Suzanne Keller ,"Beyond the ruling class .Strategic Elites in modern society", Transaction Publishers 1963
[iv] Alvin Toffler ,"Future Shock" , Bantam Book 1970
[v] Stanley Hoffmann ,"Weighing the Balance of Power" , Foreign Affairs June 1972
[vi] Paul Kennedy , "The Rise and Fall of the Great Powers" ,1987
[vii] Francis Fukuyama ,"The End of History and the Last Man ", The National interest 1989
[viii] Joseph S. Nye, "Soft Power: The Means to Success in World Politics", Carnegie Council Books 1990
[ix] H. Kellner-F.W.Hueberger with a foreword by P. L. Berger, " Hidden Technocrats The New Class and New Capitalism", Transactions Publishers 1992
[x] Samuel P. Huntington, "The Clash of civilizations?", Foreign Affairs 1993
[xi] Peter F. Drucker ,"Post Capitalist Society" Harper Business 1994
[xii] Kenichi Ohmae , The End of the Nation-State: the Rise of Regional Economies, Simon and Schuster Inc., 1995

[xiii] Stanley Hoffmann, " Clash of Globalizations" , Foreign Affairs July/August 2002

[xiv] Jacque Attali ,Une breve histoire de l'avenir" , Librairie Artheme Fayand 2006

[xv] Dominique Moisi , "The clash of emotions", Foreign Affairs January/February 2007

[xvi] Azar Gst , The Return of Authoritarian Great Powers ,July/August 2007

[xvii] Richard N,. Haas , „ The age of non polarity" ,Foreign Affairs May/June 2008

[xviii] Ulrich Beck ,"Macht und GegenMacht im Globalen Zeitalter, Suhrkamp 2009

[xix] Ian Morris, „ The west rules-for now. The patterns of history, and what they reveal about the future", Farrar Straus & Giraux 201o

[xx] Nancy Birdsall ,Francis Fukuyama The Post Washington Consensus , Foreign Affairs March/April 2011

[xxi] Gideon Rose, „Making Modernity Work. The Reconciliation of Capitalism and Democracy", ibidem 1

[xxii] Henry Kissinger ,"Diplomacy", Simon & Schuster 1994

[xxiii] The Cambridge economic history of Europe. Volume III: Economic organization and politics in the Middle Ages, Cambridge University Press 1965

Fernand Braudel,"Civilisation materielle economie et capitalism (XV-XVIII siecle),Les jeux de l'exchange ,Librerie Armand Collin 1979. Kirti N. Chaudhuri ,"Asia before Europe .Economy and civilization", Cambridge University Press 1990

Nayan Chanda, " Bound together. How traders, preachers, adventures and warriors shaped globalization", Yale Press University 2007

Roderich Ptak,"Die Marittime Seidenstrasse", C.H. Beck 2007

[xxiv] National Intelligence Council, "Global Trends 2025. A transformed world " , NIC 2008http://www.dni.gov/nic/PDF_2025/2025_Global_Trends_Final_Report.pdf
[xxv] Ibidem VIII

(Private Financial Controllers, Functional Organizations, Supervising International Organizations, Transnational Organized Crime, Regional Organizations, Private International Powerhouse)

Chap. 31- The rating index: is the end of the SA´s soft power? (3/4)

Westphalia XXI, 3-7-2012

When, (the second dimension of the historical background), is the debt the destiny of the world?

It is told that nothing new happens under the sun and this is valid also when we talk about debts and sovereigns. Unlucky we tend too often to forget that there is a world long time before internet, the end of the cold war or Bretton Woods. Kingdoms and empires default and with them banks and bankers but despite it the world has been developing. In this chapter we will place in the right contest the actual crisis shortly talking about 35 years if debts from 2001 till 2035. A travel in the past, a past that starts in the year 1826, and into a plausible future..

This travel is possible thanks to three interesting studies and a conference:

-      Joseph E. Gagnon, Marc Hinterschwiger: The global outlook for government debt over the next 25 years. Implications for the economy and public policy. (Policy analyses in International Economics N.94 /June 2011 – Peterson Institute for International Economics)

- Carmen M. Reinhart ,Kenneth S. Rogoff : A decade of Debt (Policy analyses in International Economics N.95 /September 2011 – Peterson Institute for International Economics)

- John H. Makin, Desmond Lachman, Alex J. Pollock, Global Currency War, and Endless Financial Crises: What's wrong with the International Monetary System? (March 12th 2012, conference at the AEI)
- Marius Jurgilas and Filip Žikeš[i] , Implicit intraday interest rate in the UK unsecured overnight money market ,(Work Paper N. 447 ,March 2012 Bank of England)
It seems that the debt will be a continuing vulnerability and we add that sophisticated NSA like the rating Agencies will be key actors on influencing this fragility of the State Actors.

In the WWI and during the Great Depression the most used tools to solve the crisis were the default and restructuring when the WWII debts were solved through financial repression. The bailout approach started with the 1992 Japanese domestic banking crisis that was followed by the Mexican peso crisis,(1994-5),and later by the Asian crisis with the Korean package.

In the current crisis the bailouts a approach started in the USA in the 2007 .

Logically we assist also to a more subtle form of debt restructuring and this takes the form of the so-called "financial repression".. We use the term "financial depression" as described by Edward Shaw,(1973),and Ronald McKinnon,(1973),and the pillars are : explicit or indirect caps or ceiling on interests rates particularly but not exclusively these of sovereigns, the creation and maintenance of a captive domestic audience that facilitated directed credit to the government, others common measure associated with financial repression like ,for example, the direct ownership, (China, India, the UK),or their extensive management like in Japan as well restricting entry into the financial industry and directing credit to certain industries,(Beim and Clomiris,2000).

Debts, as told, were a constant throughout ages ,continents and form of government because at some point the government finances started to rapidly deteriorate. The most recurrent source of this deterioration was the war,(the last example the Vietnam War),and during peace time it was and it is the surges in public debts.

There are many reason for these surges and this is currently happens ,for example, with the BRICS and other developing countries and not only either to improve the welfare,(Brasil, China, Indonesia...),as tool to achieve the social stability required to preserve the political order as to support the economy, (China). But this is also happening in the developed one like ,for the example, irrational subsidies to the local farmers ,(..and electors...), in the USA as well as in the EU.

To this we have also to add the (growing) tendency toward a direct government engagement in rescue operations in almost all sectors of the economy.

And last but not least the chronic inability to tax effectively or in other terms to find the money where it is. We can consider tow extremes on it. One is that of the growing illegal economy, (we describe it as RCE = real crime economy), and the second is described as a privilege for low taxation of the elites that increases that gap between the "have/haves not"[ii] .

All the three but mentioned trends ,(with the exclusion of the illegal economy),can be easily explained as an effort of the Politically Elected Elites ,(PEE), to satisfy different segments of the society ,in other terms :their electors . This a bi-partisan aptitude as, for example, Parker, (2011), explains about the USA and Lenglet and Vilain,(2012), about France.

The final consequence is a gradual debt buildup but we have not to forget that this is a characteristic also of the aftermath of banking crisis and this for over a century,(a buildup that in a more than a century long period generates an average debt rise of 86%).

3.I – The past since 1826 …

As Reinhart and Rogoff have found the constant consequences of severe financial crises were and are deep and lasting effects on asset prices, output and employment, decline of housing prices, rising of the unemployment and this extends out for 5-6 years. Unlucky this situation spreads also in countries that did not experience a major financial crisis if we consider that for them during the period 2007-2010 the debt rose by an average of 36%.

We can describe it as the financial crash-sovereign debt crisis sequence,(Reinhart & Rogoff 2011b),and this description is the consequence of the evaluation of 70 countries since 1826,(when the newly independent Latin Americas economies or the first time entered the global financial markets),through 2010.

According to Reinhart & Rogoff "*the drama that has most notably engulfed Iceland and Ireland is novel only in the orders of magnitude of the debt, not in the causes and patterns of the crisis*"
"Not the causes and the patterns of the crisis"... as we can see with the hidden debts or the private debts that become public as it was in Chile in the early '80's.

And this example introduces us to the situation were banking crises act as predictors of sovereigns debt problems. The historical experience confirms that baking crises most often either precede or coincide with sovereign debt crises.

Diaz-Alejandro,(1985),Velasco,(1987), have found the reasons for this temporal sequence in the contingent liability situation in which the government takes on massive debts from the private banks and doing so it undermines its own solvency. This is also found in Kaminsky and Reinhart,(1999),when the talk about the "twin crisis" phenomenon. The "twin crisis" is generated by banking crises that precede currency crashes and that undermine the solvency of both private and sovereign borrowers. This situation is contagious and other countries ,(like in a perverse domino), are effected. This initiates a casual chain from sovereign debt crisis to banking crisis that generates a financial repression and international capital controls and not mention that the government can force healthy banks to buy significant quantities of sovereigns,(or of debt if you prefer).

In these circumstances if a government defaults this will directly impact the banks and not only these of the interested country. At this point we faces a multidimensional crisis composed by a connected network of crises. The first dimension is national and affects the government in the country Alfa and the local banks. The second dimension is international due to the simultaneous consequences on the foreign bank´s balance sheets holder of sovereigns issued by Alpha. Their problems require the action of their governments in the countries Beta, Delta. ,Gamma that take care of their debts and this generates a growth of the debt. This growth generates an higher cost of the sovereign ... . Additionally we have to consider that no one can escape the crisis because even if a bank in the country Alpha is not over exposed to sovereign it faces the "sovereign ceiling" and this means that as corporate borrower is not rated higher than its government and this implies a higher cost to borrow in the international markets. This higher costs is not only inside the international market if we consider, for example, the intraday market in the UK..,(Jurgilas and Žike, 2012). The result will be a credit crunch for the economy and that will generate more insolvencies in the economy and this will rise the bank insolvencies and with them the need for the government to increase the debt to intervene in the system. This will made worse either the rating of the sovereigns making not only more expansive to borrow but also and also the situation of international banks holding sovereigns of the country affected by a crisis. This will generate problem of liquidity for them and all will spread the effect into a multi-dimensional, (national plus international), scale.

How can we describe this situation?

Common fundamentals? Contagion? A mix of both circumstances?

To understand it we must make a clear distinction between two kinds of shocks that generate an international transmission.

One is the shock generated by a "common shock",(for example the collapse of the "dotcoms" in the 2001 or that of the houses prices in the 2008).

The other is the "cross-linkages shock" and it is a shock generating a transmission that occurs primarily due the mechanism that are the results of an international contagion emanating from the epicenter..

We are living a "fast and furious" contagion originated by cross-linkages shock and we face a situation where the same borrowers have common creditors and this make all worst. And almost creditors that were surprised by the crises. This in a situation where short before the crisis we had a surge in capital inflow ,(a "capital flow bonanza")and rapidly rising leverage with an abrupt if not a stop in the wake of the crisis.

This scenario shows the three pillars typically found in a "fast and furious" contagion as described by Kaminsky, Reinhart and Vegh,(2003).

The epilogue is a dramatic march from high public indebtedness to sovereign default,(worst case),or restructuring.

A trend that we describe using the conclusions of the mentioned book wrote by - Carmen M. Reinhart, Kenneth S. Rogoff and based on the analysis of 44 countries in a 200 years period with 3.700 annual observations covering a wide range of political systems, institutions, exchange rate arrangements and historic circumstances : " … *high levels of debt dampen growth… the sharp run-up in public sector debt will likely prove one of the most enduring legacies of the 200709 financial crises in the USA and elsewhere.* We examine the experience of 44 countries spanning up to tow centuries of data on central government debt, inflation and growth. *Our main finding is that across both advanced countries and emerging markets ,high debt/GDP levels ,(90% and above),are associated with notably lower-growth outcomes. Much lower level of external debt/GDO ,(60%), are associated with adverse outcomes for emerging markets growth. Seldom do countries "grow" their way out of debts.*

The nonlinear response of growth to debt as debt grows toward historical boundaries is reminiscent of the " debt intolerance" phenomenon developed in Reinhart,Rogoff and Savastano,(2003). As countries hit debit intolerance ceilings, market interests' rate can begin to rise quite suddenly, forcing painful adjustment. For many if not most advanced countries, .dismissing debt concerns at this time are tantamount to ignoring the proverbial elephant in the room. So is pretending that not restructuring will be necessary. It may not be called restructuring, as not to offend the sensitivities of governments that want to pretend to find an advanced –economy solution for an emerging market style sovereign debt crisis. As in other debt crisis resolution episodes, debt buybacks and debt-equity swaps are a part of the restructuring landscape. Financial repression is not likely also to prove a politically correct term –so prudential regulation will probably provide the aegis for a return to a system more akin to what the global economy had prior to the 1980´s market –based reforms.

The process where debts are being "placed" at below-market interests rates in pension funds and other more captive domestic financial institutions is already under way in several countries to drive central banks in many emerging markets to purchase US government bonds on a large scale. ***In other words, markets for government bonds are increasingly populated by nonmarket players, calling into question the information content of bond prices relative to their underlying risk profile*** *–a common feature of financially repressed systems"*

This for the past and the for the future?

3. B) The worst scenario till 2035...

According to Gagnon and Hinterschwiger,(2011),this crisis is only accelerating the fiscal deterioration of a lot of countries generating worrisome trajectories for a number of years.

In the 2008-2009 we had a crisis generated by speculation that required a coordinate response that as lasting consequence has not the solution of the crisis but the rising of deficits to records level for peacetime.

We avoid a new Great Depression to find not growth but the **Great Indebtedness** that will last for years.

The core problem is a lack of credibility that takes the form of higher and higher interest rates for the sovereign. A trend that is spreading and that will also include a country like Germany as logic consequences that its markets are going down and with "Agenda 2010" the growth is export and not by the internal demand generated. In other terms : till the world buys Made in Germany Agenda 2012 can work but it the world will buy less the system will get on troubles.

Additionally the demography seems to play against even if we do not agree with the negative forecasts by Gagnon and Hinterschwiger in the "Global Aging Preparedness Index" published by the Center of Strategic International Studies and the insurance company Jackson,(2010)[iii]

Public Health Benefits to the Elderly, as a Percent of GDP in 2007 and 2040: Baseline versus Alternative "Excess Cost Growth" Scenarios*				
Country		Baseline Convergence to Per Capita GDP + 1.0%	Alternative 1 Convergence to Per Capita GDP +2.0%	Alternative 2 No Convergence
	2007	2040	2040	2040
Australia	2.7	6.1	5.6	10.6
Brazil	1.4	5.4	5.0	8.3
Canada	3.6	7.7	7.0	7.3
Chile	2.3	3.3	3.0	3.3
China	0.6	2.6	2.5	2.4
France	4.6	9.2	8.5	10.0
Germany	4.1	7.9	6.7	8.4
India	0.2	0.9	0.9	0.8
Italy	3.4	6.7	6.2	6.6
Japan	4.6	7.9	6.4	6.8
Korea	1.6	5.4	5.0	4.9
Mexico	0.7	3.9	2.8	2.2
Netherlands	3.9	8.5	7.9	8.3
Poland	3.7	3.7	3.6	4.4
Russia	2.5	3.5	3.3	3.3
Spain	3.1	6.9	6.4	7.7
Sweden	4.9	6.7	6.2	5.7
Switzerland	4.6	7.4	7.0	8.3
UK	4.0	7.5	6.9	8.4
US	4.2	9.3	8.8	11.1

*Excess cost growth equals the growth rate in age-adjusted per capita spending minus the growth rate in per capita GDP.

As the table show even in the worst scenario we can consider that the mentioned countries **have the resources to pay their welfare and this despite a lot of alarmism. It is hard to believe that Italy cannot afford to pay for it the 6.7% of its GDP or that the USA the 11.1%.**

This authoritative study made by Jackson, Howe and Nakshima concludes that:" *Clearly, global aging poses a daunting economic and social challenge. Many fast-aging countries, especially in the developed world, seem to face a choice between relieving the growing fiscal burden on the young and maintaining adequate incomes for the old. meanwhile, in many developing countries, the choice seems to be just the opposite: whether to impose a new fiscal burden on the young in order to relieve the growing vulnerability of the old. **Yet just as clearly, there are many strategies available to address the challenge and not all involve painful trade-offs**. Two in particular, extending work lives and increasing funded retirement savings, can be win-win solutions that help provide the old the security that* *they have earned while ensuring the young the future of expanding economic opportunity that they deserve.*

Although this report has focused on the importance of government policy choices in confronting the aging challenge, businesses also have a critical role to play—by educating workers about retirement security, by encouraging long-term savings, and by restructuring their workplaces to accommodate older workers. As our societies age, individuals and families inevitably will also have to take greater personal responsibility in planning for old age.

With much of the world still reeling from the global economic crisis, many policy leaders may conclude that now is not the right time to address the long-term challenge of global aging. This would be a mistake. In fact, the economic crisis has made timely action even more urgent than before. On the one hand, the crisis has drastically reduced the room that many countries have to accommodate rising old-age dependency costs, and so has brought their day of fiscal reckoning forward. On the other hand, the market meltdown has left many elders more vulnerable. There is also the critical issue of confidence. Both the public and the markets increasingly worry that governments have lost control over their fiscal future. Taking credible steps to address the long-term aging challenge may thus be a necessary part of addressing the near-term economic challenge as well."

This report evaluates one of most lasting consequences of the economic crises that is seems started on 9/15 that is related to the new political roles of the Credit Rating Agencies, (CRA), that we consider as a Not State Actor ,(NSA) ,described as one of the 24 forms of NSA´s according to the Paolo Dealberti's ´s classification[i].

We do not believe that this crisis started with 9/15 but that 9/15 was the moment where the system imploded.

We think that all started in the 60′s, (George Packer is telling 1978[ii]),with an elite of brilliant " eggs heads" that were advisors of the White House. In any case is a social trend before and beyond an economic one and it is deeper and more sophisticated as well as complex than so-called "neoconservative" and "neoliberal" revolution of the ′80′s. More sophisticated and complex because on worldwide bases with different forms and nuances that sometime has the form of political protests ,(from the Arab Spring to the Indignatos in Spain or the Referendari anti-nucleare,(also with the support of established political party like Italia Dei Valori), in Italy, the Occupy Wall Street Movement in the USA or Die Piraten in Germany[iii] or the around 280.000 riots in China[iv]), and sometime that of a deep rethinking of social aptitudes[v].
The emerging force inside the economic and political crisis is that of a social class that we describe as the "**1st cosmopolitan and transversal new bourgeois**". Something *"more and beyond the myth"* of **the world middle class**[vi] and we develop it in a future report.

In our report we focus on the geopolitical dimension and we talk about actors that existed long time before the PWO and that are existing also today. : the Not State Actors. And inside the NSA′s we find an important part of the 1stcosmopolitan and transversal new bourgeois that we mentioned before.

We will evaluate the NSA′s inside the actual tensions with the PWO actors*pour excellence:* the State Actors.

Notes:

[i] Paolo Dealberti, "The 24 forms of NSA′s and their classification as genetically authoritarian/ not genetically authoritarian", classified internal document 2009

[ii] George Packer, "The broken contract", Foreign Affairs Vol. 90 N. 6 2011 but also Suzanne Keller ,"Beyond the ruling class .Strategic Elites in modern society", (note III) Hansfired Kellner – Frank W. Huberger ,(note XI)

[iii] Indignatos = Outraged a movement of the social inequality in Spain , Referendari anti nucleare = supporters of the referendum against the nuclear energy, Die Piraten = The Pirates a new party in Germany that is entering in one regional Council after the other.

[iv] Gordon G. Chang , "The Coming Collapse of China: 2012 Edition ", Foreign Policy Dec. 29 2011http://www.foreignpolicy.com/articles/2011/12/29/the_co ming_collapse_of_china_2012_edition?page=0,1&wpisrc=ob insite

[v] Monocle ,Issue 49 Vol 5 , Dec. 2011/ Jan.2012 Courrier International , Revolution ,revelation ou regression ? Tendences 2012", Horse-serie Tendences Dec. 2011

[vi] Karen Harris, Austin Kim and Andrew Schwedel,"The Great Eight: Trillion-Dollar Growth Trends to 2020",Bain & Company 2011

http://www.bain.com/publications/articles/eight-great-trillion-dollar-growth-trends-to-2020.aspx

Paolo Dealberti," World middle-class : how a self-fuelling "myth" could be used by someone to affect our democracies " ,Prosumerzen 2011

http://prosumerzen.net/2011/09/26/world-middle-class-how-a-self-fuelling-%E2%80%9Cmyth%E2%80%9D-could-be-used-by-someone-to-affect-our-democracies/

Homi Kharas.,"The emerging middle class in developing countries" ,OECD Report Oct. 2010

(Private Financial Controllers, Functional Organizations, Supervising International Organizations, Transnational Organized Crime, Regional Organizations, Private International Powerhouse)

Chap. 32 - The rating index: is the end of the SA´s soft power? (4/4)

Westphalia XXI, 5-7-2012

Who? The tensions between the PWO State Actors and the NSA called Credit Rating Agencies

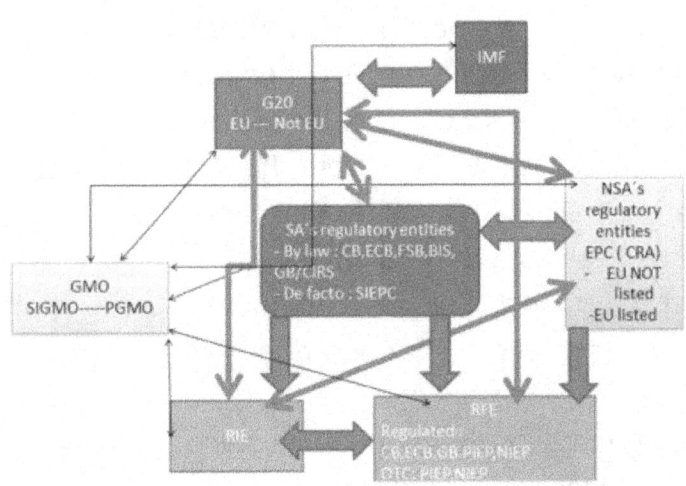

(Interactions between the Real Industrial Economy, the Real Financial Economy inside the financial and economic crisis since 2008 - ©2012 all rights reserved Paolo Dealberti)

This report evaluates one of most lasting consequences of the economic crises that is seems started on 9/15 that is related to the new political roles of the Credit Rating Agencies, (CRA), that we consider as a Not State Actor ,(NSA) ,described as one of the 24 forms of NSA´s according to the Paolo Dealberti's ´s classification[i].
We do not believe that this crisis started with 9/15 but that 9/15 was the moment where the system imploded.

We think that all started in the 60´s, (George Packer is telling 1978[ii]),with an elite of brilliant " eggs heads" that were advisors of the White House. In any case is a social trend before and beyond an economic one and it is deeper and more sophisticated as well as complex than so-called "neoconservative" and "neoliberal" revolution of the ´80´s. More sophisticated and complex because on worldwide bases with different forms and nuances that sometime has the form of political protests ,(from the Arab Spring to the Indignatos in Spain or the Referendari anti-nucleare in Italy, the Occupy Wall Street Movement in the USA or Die Piraten in Germany[iii] or the around 280.000 riots in China[iv]), and sometime that of a deep rethinking of social aptitudes[v].
The emerging force inside the economic and political crisis is that of a social class that we describe as the "**1st cosmopolitan and transversal new bourgeois**". **Something "*more and beyond the myth*" of the world middle class**[vi] and we develop it in a future report.

In our report we focus on the geopolitical dimension and we talk about actors that existed long time before the PWO and that are existing also today. : the Not State Actors. And inside the NSA´s we find an important part of the 1stcosmopolitan and transversal new bourgeois that we mentioned before.

We will evaluate the NSA´s inside the actual tensions with the PWO actors*pour excellence:* the State Actors.

3.1 The NSA´s before and after the PWO

In the world before as well as long after the Pax of Westphalia and its order the rule was that of the coexistence between the NSA´s and what at that time represented a power comparable to that of a modern SA.

Some examples:

- Let´s imagine a multinational company ,(MLC),that has the following privileges:
- The monopoly in each country where is located

- The control of the harbors in its own country

- Once a tax,(custom), is paid its government has not any other right about its actions in the hub as well as in the host country

- Its managers have a power like that of the army officer

- If you work for this company you can avoid the military duty

- This company can have its own navy and army and if it uses the force it is accountable only to its government and not to that of the country where the force was used

- It can keep secret both the balance sheet and the name of the stockholders

And now let´s imagine that pirates based in Madagascar are talking with the head of an European government to establish a base in Europe because they want to supply know-how, man power and money to create one of these NSA-multinationals in Europe.

This is neither the next 007 movie nor a novel. This is history. The list of privileges was the standard for **the multinationals in the XVI-XIX** and we know them as the "East /West India Companies". The pirates were in contact with the King Cal XII of Sweden in 1715 and only the death of the king stopped the project. It seems that there nothing of new under the sun and that ,when we are talking about the Not State Actors /NSA , we are "simply" forgetting two centuries of history. In the XVII – XIX were created the following multinationals
- East India Company , UK, 31-12-1600 till 1-11-1874

- Veernigde Ost Indiche, (East India Company),Holland, 1602-1800

- La Compagnie Française des indes Orientales , (East India Company),France; 14/1/1731-1813

- Svenska Ostindiska Coamaniet , (East India Company),Sweden, 1718

- East India Company of Denmark, 1630

- Western India Company of Holland, 3/6/1621- 1791

- Western India Company of France, 1635, (with a fleet of 45 gunned ships), till 1674

- We can add to this list also the Canadian and Russian companies that controlled the hunting in N. America and the railways companies in the USA in the XIX

From the XVII till the XIX these companies had an economic, financial, political and military power that is not equaled in the XXI. De facto they and their governments were the real masters of the world or, to be more direct, they were the only alternative powers to the state actors. But most important: they were NSA´s.

- The catholic Church since the III AC
- The medieval *Gilde*. The organization of workers, merchants as well as members of the *"professioni liberali",(for exp. lawyers),* inside each European town in the Middle age and in the Renaissance.
- The structure "town-village-market" since the Han Kingdom ,(II BC),in China
- The Samurai in Japan till the Meinji reform
- The legal and religious Schools in the Arab and Ottoman Empires

- The double structure of power between Mandarins and Eunuchs in China since IV BC till 1912

Actors able to shape the world and to create something equivalent to our civil society and able to produce a document like the Magna Charta[vii].

3.1.A   The world today

It seems that there is nothing new under the sun also in the second decade of the XXI when we talk about the relation between NSA´s and SA´s after 9/15. The NSA´s are described under the Paolo Dealberti´s " The 24 forms of NSA´s and their classification as genetically authoritarian/ not genetically authoritarian" classification,*(note:you can find an up-top-date version ar www.appealpower.com).*

The global structure of the world economy is composed by three dimensions:

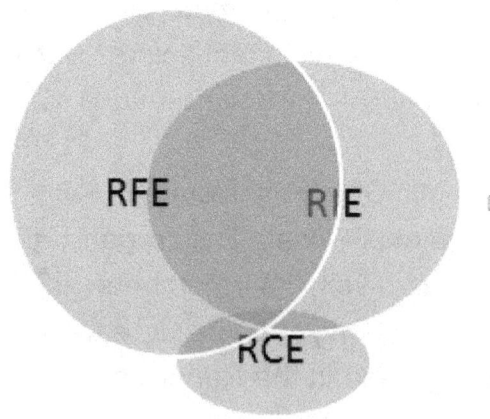

- The **Real Industrial Economy, (RIE):** it includes all produced, traded and sold inside the primary, secondary and tertiary sectors but not services and products related to the financial industry. From what traded in a small rural village to intra-company trading to build-up a satellite. The Forbes World Top 500 offers a list of the main protagonists. Inside the RIE we have different forms of NSA´s[xv] but we do not consider them for our report.

- **The Real Financial Economy ,(RFE)[xvi]:** either we decide that the backbone of the current financial infrastructure of the world born in the*Fiera del Danaro* in Piacenza ,(1579),or with the stock exchange in Amsterdam,(1622),we see that today we are simply and only living the last episode of a secular trend. There is nothing under the sun also either when we talk about the speculation and the so-called financial leverage that seems able to cut any link between the real and financial economy. In Amsterdam people were used to buy the swap for contract for a black tulip with a luxury coach with four horses,(it is like that today you buy a swap for a black tulip with the contract for a Ferrari...). In the stock exchange in London ,(only twenty years later), the stock market was 50 times bigger than the "real economy",(today we talk about a 20:1 leverage...). In order to be able to better understand the forces and real dynamics of the financial market that we forget the useless distinction between ,(a so-called), "real" economy and a so-called "virtual /financial" one. The financial economy is a real one with its own rules, needs and from of money ,if not currency, that for the most is working and developing inside the OTC markets.

- The **Real Criminal Economy, (RCE)**: the third component of the world economy is the criminal one that represents around 25-28% of the world GDP.

It is a parallel world that overlaps with the legal economy either because of the money laundering and because of the influence of violence,(from rackets in Palermo, prostitution in Hamburg, drug gangs in Washington to the hijacking of a container ship by pirates in the African Horn). A world with its own parallel and efficient systems to transfer money around the globe ,(Black Hawala).Also this dimension has its own NSA's[xvii] but they are not relevant inside our report. And, last but not least, a dimension with an incredible power if , for example, we consider that :

- The Italian Mafias, (sacra corona unita , mafia, camorra, n´drangheta) , generate more than 120 billion €/year making this cartel one of the biggest company in Europe

- If the biggest criminal cartels in Russia, China, Italy, Turkey, Nigeria, Mexico, USA, Israel, Colombia, India, Albania, Bolivia, and Brasil[xviii] will joint their not yet invested financial resources represent the biggest source of cash of the planet. A lot richer than the SWF´s of the IFSWF.

3.2 The tensions between SA´s and NSA´s

Unlucky there is a false as well negative "mythology" when we talk about the NSA´s because too much are compared with grey if not black powers. This perception is totally wrong because:

a) As told before the NSA´s are the rule inside the international politics, economy as well as inside the social landscape since centuries

b) Only few of them are to be considered negative and dangerous.

Prosumerzen classifies[xix] them as "**genetically /not genetically authoritarian**" and all the NSA´s, (private as well as state influenced). The risk for the democracy it is not stake and it must not be the argument of this report. The NSA´s , (banks, hedge funds, credit rating agencies ,global media outlet), are not run by a group of technocrats that want to subvert the democracy and impose some kind of "techno-dictatorship". The genetically authoritarian NSA´s belong to other dimensions of the international arena like these of the international politics or international crime. That does not means that if the markets will fall down the economic nightmare that will follow will not rise the chance for illiberal, nationalistic, racist, fundamentalist forces to menace our liberty. **The risk is high as never before since 1939 and we are here to win this battle but, again, the NSA´s in the financial world "*as and because*" NSA´s are not the problem on itself**.

Before that we evaluate how inside the current situation the Credit Rating Agencies /CRA´s, *(since now : Economic Private Controllers/EPC)*,can affect the SA´s soft power it is important :

I) To know the outlook 2012 for the financial services industry

II)   How the main global players are acting and for this we evaluate the FBS prescriptions, the EU prescriptions, the Standard & Poor´s feedback to the EU, how a SIEPC like Dagong ,(China), acts and the new ,(released on 31-1-12),index created by the Indian Dept. of Finance, (a Governmental Branch ,GB), and called CRIS.

This will be discussed in the next 6 chapters and in the last we will back to how the NSA´s can affect the NSA´s soft power inside the financial markets.

Notes:

[i] Paolo Dealberti, " The 24 forms of NSA´s and their classification as genetically authoritarian/ not genetically authoritarian", classified internal document 2009

[ii] George Packer, "The broken contract", Foreign Affairs Vol. 90 N. 6 2011 but also Suzanne Keller ,"Beyond the ruling class .Strategic Elites in modern society", (note III) Hansfired Kellner – Frank W. Huberger ,(note XI)

[iii] Indignatos = Outraged a movement of the social inequality in Spain , Referendari anti nucleare = supporters of the referendum against the nuclear energy, Die Piraten = The Pirates a new party in Germany that is entering in one regional Council after the other.

[iv] Gordon G. Chang , "The Coming Collapse of China: 2012 Edition ", Foreign   Policy   Dec.   29 2011http://www.foreignpolicy.com/articles/2011/12/29/the_coming_collap se_of_china_2012_edition?page=0,1&wpisrc=obinsite

[v] Monocle ,Issue 49 Vol 5 , Dec. 2011/ Jan.2012

Courrier International , Revolution ,revelation ou regression ? Tendences 2012", Horse-serie Tendences Dec. 2011

[vi] Karen Harris, Austin Kim and Andrew Schwedel,"The Great Eight: Trillion-Dollar Growth Trends to 2020",Bain & Company 2011http://www.bain.com/publications/articles/eight-great-trillion-dollar-growth-trends-to-2020.aspx
Paolo Dealberti," World middle-class : how a self-fuelling "myth" could be used by someone to affect our democracies " ,Prosumerzen 2011http://prosumerzen.net/2011/09/26/world-middle-class-how-a-self-fuelling-%E2%80%9Cmyth%E2%80%9D-could-be-used-by-someone-to-affect-our-democracies/
Homi Kharas.,"The emerging middle class in developing countries" ,OECD Report Oct. 2010

[vii] Eric T. Kasper ," The influence of the Magna Carta in limiting Executive Power in the War on Terror", Political Science Quarterly Vol. 126 N.4 Winter 2011-2012
[viii] http://ec.europa.eu/internal_market/securities/docs/agencies/list_en.pdf
[ix] A list,(alphabetical order), of the Top 15 CRA, (The Top 16 include also Dagong). Prosumerzen monitors them in the editorial section " The 16" ,(www.prosumerzen.net)
[x] Ibidem XXXi
[xi] Prosumerzen monitors them inside the editorial section " Soulmakers"
[xii] These banks plus RBS are monitored inside the Prosumerzen ´s editorial section "Windhandel" as the most influential banks in the world due to theor dominant position inside the financial engineering
[xiii] The source is the Barclays database about hedge funds.

[xiv] We use the Dealberti´s classification,(ibidem XXIV). Prosumerzen is monitoring on weekly basis the mentioned NSA´s ,(www.prosumerzen.net)

[xv] Ibidem XXIV

[xvi] Prosumerzen is monitoring the most sophisticated actors Barclays, Jp Morgan ,Citigroup, Bank of America ,Credit Suisse inside the editorial section "Windhandel"-

[xvii] Ibidem XXIV

[xviii] In Prosumerzen we call them the „ C- G13" Criminal G13

[xix] Ibidem XXIV

(Form of NSA: Multinationals)

Chap. 33 - Multinationals like Not State Actors

April 20, 2011

Let's imagine a multinational company, (MLC) that has the following privileges:

- The monopoly in each country where is located

- The control of the harbors in its own country

- Once a tax is paid its government has not any other right about its action

- Its managers have a power like that of the army officer of its country

- If you work for this company you can avoid the military duty

- This company can have its own navy and army and if it uses the force it is accountable only to its government and not to that of the country where the force was used

- It can keep secret either the balance sheet and the name of the stockholders

And now let's imagine that pirates based in Madagascar are talking with the head of a European government to establish a base in Europe because they want to supply know-how, man power and money to create one of these multinationals in Europe.

This is neither the next 007 movie nor a romance. **This is history.**

The list of privileges was the standard for the multinationals in the XVI-XIX and we know them as "East /West India Companies". The pirates were in contact with the king Cal XII of Sweden in 1715 and only the death of the king stopped the project.
It seems that there nothing of new under the sun and that, when **we are talking about the Not State Actors /NSA, we are forgetting two centuries of history**

In the XVII – XIX were created the following multinationals

- East India Company , UK, 31-12-1600 till 1-11-1874

- Veering Ost Indiche, (East India Company),Holland, 1602-1800

- La Compagnie Française des indes Orientales , (East India Company),France; 14/1/1731-1813

- Svenska Ostindiska Coamaniet , (East India Company),Sweden, 1718

- East India Company of Denmark , 1630

- Western India Company of Holland , 3/6/1621- 1791

- Western India Company of France , 1635, (with a fellt of 45 gunned ships),till 1674

- We can add to this list also the Canadian and Russian companies that controlled the hunting in N. America and the railways companies in the USA in the XIX

From the XVII till the XIX these companies had an economic, financial, political and military power that has not equal in the XXI

De facto they and their government were the real masters of the world or, to be more direct, they were the only alternative powers to the state actors. And they were NSA.

NSA acting in partnership or against the international organized crime structures of that period, (smugglers and pirates), and that used what we today describe as "corporate insurgency/counterinsurgency".

They had private navies and armies, (today we describe them as Private Security Forces /PSF), as well as their intelligence.

They had a great influence in the internal politics of the "hosting countries" as well as in the "home countries", (even if they used different means to achieve it).

They worked in perfect synergy with "banque d´affairs" with a real financial power that no contemporary SWF has.

They had their own foreign policy that was not always the same of their governments.

An interesting example is the "Opium War „and Professor Ian Morris in his last international bestseller describes it:

"This was not the British Empire´s finest hour. Contemporary analogies are never precise ,but it was rather as if in response to the US Drug Enforcement Agency making a major bust, the Tijuana cartel , (my note : in this case in the analogy the Tijuan cartel is the East India Company),*prevailed on the Mexican Government to shoot its way into San Diego demanding that the White House reimburse the drug lords for the street value of the confiscated cocaine,(plus interests and carriage charge),as well as paying the costs of the military expedition. Imagine too, that while it was in the neighborhood, a Mexican fleet seized Catalina Island,* (my note in this case there analogy is with the size of Hong Kong), *as a base for future operations and threatened to blockade Washington until the Congress gave the Tijuana drug lords monopoly rights in Los Angeles, Chicago and New York*" (Ian Morris, Why the west rules for now. The patterns of history, and what they reveal about the future", page 7 – Farrar, Straus & Giroux /New York 2010)

These words by one of the best modern historian describe a situation where we find states within the states when we talk about foreign policy.

No contemporary multinational has an equivalent power.

The history of these multinationals is interesting to better understand the NSA in the XXI.

Unlucky today we talk too much about the globalization forgetting that it started in the middle age. Or at least the modern globalization if we consider that Rome traded with China and that in the IV BC the custom of Rome recorded fruits and plants from…Australia. Maybe we have forgot the Fernand Braudel´s brilliant pages about the Mediterranean in the Renaissance and these of Kirti N. Chaudhuri about Asia before the Portuguese domination , (I).

If we put the globalization in its historical track we can better understand the future.

These companies were de facto nations within nations with a power that no XXI multinational have but despite that they failed and the state actors are still here.

They failed because of the competition, (the French East India Company lost vs. that of Amsterdam).

But they failed also because the governments, (the state actors), decided to take back their powers and prerogatives and crashed down the power of the companies.
From the Government of India Act 1858, (London crashed down the East India Company), to the US anti-trust law at the end of the XIX, (Washington crashed down the American monopolists).

If we think that today is too late it is better to remember the destiny of ATT when it was a monopolist.

Or what is going on in the oil industry.

The "7 sisters" are only a souvenir of the past. Today the

75% of the oil industry and of reserves are controlled by state companies, (we suggest to read Ian Bremmer/2009). And a power shift is going on also in the financial world where the SWF are state controlled financial power houses.

Historia magistrae vitae...if we start to read history we can better understand our future.

In the next article we talk about another protagonist of the NSA in the XXI: the international organized crimes operating from failed states.

We will talk about a four years long war in Africa where the USA and some European powers were involved.

It was...**1801...**

Notes:
(I) about the globalization in the middle age Jacques Attali,"Une breve historie de l'avenir", Librerie Arthem Fayard/2006. About the globalization in older time Nayan Chanda, "Bound together how traders, preachers, adventures and warriors shaped globalization, Yale University Press/2007. If interested in the trade in the old Rome J. Innes Miller, „The spice trade in the Roman Empire ", Oxford University Press/1969. About the Indian Ocean before the Portuguese domination in Kirti N. Chaudhuri,"Asia before Europe. Economy and civilization of the Indian Ocean from the rise of Islam to 1750", Oxford Univ. Press/1994

(Form of NSA: Transnational Organized Crime, States Within Failed States)

Chap 34 - US, European Powers vs. Pirates in Africa

April 22, 2011

1- The historical Background

The Pirates are based in Africa and the USA with other European powers is fighting them since four years. The goal is to eradicate them and to free the seas for navigation and trade.
It seems something we know, is it?

But in this case the pirates are not in Somalia but in North Africa, (Alger, Tunis, Tripoli), and they are called or Barbary Pirates. They were able to size villages till Iceland not mention about their attacks against coastal villages and towns in Scotland, England, Italy, Spain, France, and Portugal. Based in autonomous dependencies of the Ottoman Empire, de facto "failed states areas", they were free to attack anyone they wanted. They were the backbone of an international network of organized crime engaged on smuggling as well as on selling slaves, (they captured between 800.000 – 1.250.000 people to sell)

The European powers are France, the UK, Holland, Italy, Spain but also the USA under President Jefferson.

The problem started in the XVI and lasted till 1830 when France occupied Alger.

To be honest the continuation of piracy was assisted by competition among European powers. France encouraged the pirates against Spain, and later Britain and Holland supported them against France. By the second half of the 17th century the greater European naval powers were able to strike back effectively enough to intimidate the Barbary States into making peace with them. However, those countries' commercial interests then benefited from the impact of continuing attacks on their competitors, and as a result there was little interest in imposing a more general cessation of corsair activity.

During this period flourished also a lucrative business run by what we today could describe as private security forces, (PSF) and this day were called Privateers. A privateer is a private person or ship authorized by a government by letters of marquee to attack foreign shipping during wartime. Privatizing was a way of mobilizing armed ships and sailors without having to spend public money or commit naval officers. They were, essentially, a Renaissance-era equivalent to the corporate and independent "military contractors" of today. The cost was borne by investors hoping to profit from prize money earned from captured cargo and vessels. The proceeds would be distributed among the privateer's investors, officers and crew. It has been argued that privatizing was a less destructive and wasteful form of warfare, because the goal was to capture ships rather than to sink them. Privateers were part of naval warfare from the 16th to the 19th century. Some privateers have been particularly influential in the annals of history, (for example: Barbarossa Hayreddin Pasha, Sir Francis Drake, Alonso de Contreras under the banner of the Order of Malta, Ephraim Sturdivant ...). Sometimes, the vessels would be commissioned into regular service as warships. The crew of a privateer might be treated as prisoners of war by the enemy country if captured.

Inside this scenario the United States made its first attempt to fight an overseas battle to protect its private citizens by building an international coalition against an unconventional enemy. Then the enemies were pirates and piracy. The focus of the United States and a proposed international coalition was the Barbary Pirates of North Africa. International coalition...something we knew....

As we know that to protect the sea lines is and was a vital interest. And for this reason after the United States won its independence in the treaty of 1783, it had to protect its own commerce against dangers such as the Barbary pirates. As early as 1784 Congress followed the tradition of the European shipping powers and appropriated $80,000 as tribute to the Barbary States, directing its ministers in Europe, Thomas Jefferson and John Adams, to begin negotiations with them. Trouble began the next year, in July 1785, when Algerians captured two American ships and the Dey of Algiers held their crews of twenty-one people for a ransom of nearly $60,000. Jefferson as Minister to France opposed but his plan for an international coalition foundered on the shoals of indifference and a belief that it was cheaper to pay the tribute than fight a war. The United States' relations with the Barbary States continued to revolve around negotiations for ransom of American ships and sailors and the payment of annual tributes or gifts. Even though Secretary of State Jefferson declared to Thomas Barclay, American consul to Morocco, in a May 13, 1791, letter of instructions for a new treaty with Morocco that it is "lastly our determination to prefer war in all cases to tribute under any form, and to any people whatever," the United States continued to negotiate for cash settlements. In 1795 alone the United States was forced to pay nearly a million dollars in cash, naval stores, and a frigate to ransom 115 sailors from the Dey of Algiers. Annual gifts were settled by treaty on Algiers, Morocco, Tunis, and Tripoli. Then he became President of the USA 1801. Immediately he refused to accede to Tripoli's demands for an immediate payment of

$225,000 and an annual payment of $25,000. The pasha of Tripoli then declared war on the United States. Although as secretary of state and vice president he had opposed developing an American navy capable of anything more than coastal defense, President Jefferson dispatched a squadron of naval vessels to the Mediterranean. As he declared in his first annual message to Congress: "To this state of general peace with which we have been blessed, one only exception exists. Tripoli, the least considerable of the Barbary States, had come forward with demands unfounded either in right or in compact, and had permitted itself to denounce war, on our failure to comply before a given day. The style of the demand admitted but one answer. I sent a small squadron of frigates into the Mediterranean. . . ." The American show of force quickly awed Tunis and Algiers into breaking their alliance with Tripoli. The humiliating loss of the frigate Philadelphia and the capture of her captain and crew in Tripoli in 1803, criticism from his political opponents, and even opposition within his own cabinet did not deter Jefferson from his chosen course during four years of war. The aggressive action of Commodore Edward Preble (1803-4) forced Morocco out of the fight and his five bombardments of Tripoli restored some order to the Mediterranean. However, it was not until 1805, when an American fleet under Commodore John Rogers and a land force raised by an American naval agent to the Barbary powers, Captain William Eaton, threatened to capture Tripoli and install the brother of Tripoli's pasha on the throne, that a treaty brought an end to the hostilities. Negotiated by Tobias Lear, former secretary to President Washington and now consul general in Algiers, the treaty of 1805 still required the United States to pay a ransom of $60,000 for each of the sailors held by the Dey of Algiers, and so it went without Senatorial consent until April 1806. Nevertheless, Jefferson was able to report in his sixth annual message to Congress in December 1806 that in addition to the successful completion of the Lewis and Clark expedition, "The states on the coast of Barbary seem generally disposed at present to respect our peace and friendship." In fact, it was not until the second war with

Algiers, in 1815, that naval victories by Commodores William Bainbridge and Stephen Decatur led to treaties ending all tribute payments by the United States. European nations continued annual payments until the 1830s. However, international piracy in Atlantic and Mediterranean waters declined during this time under pressure from the Euro-American nations, who no longer viewed pirate states as mere annoyances during peacetime and potential allies during war.

2- Today

Failed states, international coalition and related problems, international organized crime, opportunism and interests of the players to control the pirates, PSF, ransoms, military expedition, special forces, (the Marines were used in Tripoli as in their anthem ..."from the beach of Tripoli to..."), No State Actors vs. State Actors but also NSA allied with SA and ... money laundering and more.

It seems today is it?

It was more than 200 years ago. Again, it seems nothing new under the sun. Yesterday,(I), we mentioned multinationals as NSA and today we talk about the organized crime as NSA and in both situations it was centuries ago and for a period of 2 or 3 hundred years.

Why?

Historia magistra vitae... again we are over evaluating and misunderstanding the trends. Nothing is new but all has its own new dimension because the XXI is not the XVI or the XIX.

It is time to stop to use term like " new", " it never happened" to camouflage our abyssal historical ignorance and to consider it for what it is.an evolution . Not more, not less.

And if it is an evolution we can identify its own track and inside it to solve the problem.

It will be not easy and not in a short time but it was done…and we can solve it again.

Note :

(I)http://prosumerzen.wordpress.com/2011/04/20/multinationals-as-no-state-actors-multinazionali-come-no-state-actors-derss/

Form of NSA: Private Financial Controllers, Functional Organizations,

Supervising International Organizations, Transnational Organized Crime,

Regional Organizations, Private International Powerhouse)

Chap.35 - NSA vs. SA: rumors of a new episode of their war. This time, (2011), inside the financial market (1)

May 10, 2011

For some aspects with the Equites in the old Rome, the merchants in Cartago and even in Athens during Pericles we had strong economic and financial powers able to act as NSA.

During the Middle Age the *Comuni* and the free Towns were Towns within a State, (were the state was an empire), and for that reason the NSA of that age.
Later was the time of the economic alliances like the
Hanseatic League or of the East Indian Companies, (I).

From a sociopolitical point of view the "tea Party" in Boston was the origin of the National Liberation Movement, (another kind of NSA, for an exhaustive description of the existing 21 kinds of NSA see at II), that made the revolution against the English Crown.

The "*Jeu de Paume movement*", on 20 June 1789 short before the French Revolution, can be described as the "civil society" of that time.

Today, among others. We face NSA acting like a National Liberation Movements, (NLM), in Libya. A NLM that will rise as international powerhouse in Africa not thanks to the oil that will control but to a SWF, (III).

This war has different faces and dimensions and different goals and, logically, different players.

One of these dimensions is the war inside the financial world and this interests **on of the most sophisticated, (if not the most),** of the NSA´s.

The last chapter of this war, (another episode is, for example, the collapse of the Hedge Funds TLCM in the 1998), was 15/11 and the related financial crisis since 2008. This chapter ended on 25-09-2009 in Pittsburgh and the State Actors, (the G20), were the winners.

Why?
Simply and only because States were able to put the money on the table and to save the banks.

Despite the so-called power of the "virtual and trans-national markets" no NSA, (read private actor), was able to organize a "GX" of NSA´s able to collect the funds, (using bonds and shares as well as derivate …), inside the multi trillions dollars market and to save the banks. **No one but the SA has the credibility to do it and no NSA had the power and credibility to ask to the markets to fund it.**

Credibility?

From Parmalat to the banks and financial institutions that originated the 15/11 crisis no one, at that time, could trust a lot the "private watch dogs, (S&P, Moody´s .... All NSA in the dimension of "Private Controller/PC"), and trust any other private "white knight "to be able to solve the situation.

The request was for a force able to avoid the bankruptcy of the system. **This was a request for a vacuum to fulfill with a political power**.

The Financial NSA´s, despite the wealth of the market and their uncontrolled power inside it, had not the credibility to act as a "political actor" and to solve the problem. The States had this political credibility.

Again it was not a matter of money but of credibility. The NSA lost.

Logically this is only one of the perspectives that someone can use to read the 2008 crisis but it has its logic.

We think that on 19.4.11 we saw a signal of new tensions among them. S&P downgrade the USA bond. This week, as we told in our SWF Weekly Monitor, (IV), another interesting signal:

"If the United States loses its AAA sovereign rating, a top official at Singapore sovereign wealth fund GIC said on Monday, we back to face a world crisis. That was told by GIC Deputy Chairman Tony Tan during a conference to mark the fund´s 30th anniversary:"We face the possibility of another major financial and economic crisis if the world's risk-free asset, hitherto U.S. bonds, loses its AAA credit rating in a disorderly manner. GIC, also known as the Government of Singapore Investment Corp, manages around $300 billion in assets and is one of the world's largest sovereign wealth funds. About 36 percent of its funds

*were invested in the United States as of March 2010, according to GIC's last report. Separately, Singapore Prime Minister Lee Hsien Loong said he did not expect U.S. President Barack Obama to tackle the country's huge deficit until after presidential elections in 2012, in a sign of growing global unease about the U.S. economy. The Singapore prime minister said Standard & Poor's recent warning that it may cut the United States AAA sovereign rating has so far not affected U.S. government bond yields, but has created uncertainty as it is unclear what other currency could become a new anchor for the global economy. **The U.S. did not lack the resources to solve its deficit problems**"*

And this is the point: the USA do not lack the resources and please back to the 1998 when, after 8 years of budget control, the USA had a surplus and was considering to buy its own residual debt. Then 9/11 and the Bush Jr. financial administration….
The USA is going to this virtuoso track.

We do not think that we will see a new war and that the dollar, for the next future, will lose its role.

Why? Because it will be easy to do it but no one wants it.

Easy?

We have three dimensions where the dollar con is substitute only if a political wish wants it.

Situation 1: China

China sells in dollar. The day China will sell in yuan the dollar will lose an interesting part of its power

Situation 2: Oil & Gas

The oil and gas are traded in dollars. Why no one is asking for a different currency? For example President Chavez can substitute his "anti-western rhetoric" with a real politic tool asking to be paid with its own currency....

Russia instead to ask for a not clear basket of currencies as the " new currency" can use the brilliant minds inside its world class universities to create this basket and then to ask to be paid with that currency...

.

Iran, instead to run to be able to set a date for its bomb, could ask to China and others to be paid with its own currency. And then to pay the gasoline that imports with a price that is around 25% higher of the world price using the same currency... it will be interesting to see how many seller Teheran will find....

Situation 3: Financial Markets

There are rumors about a new currency, for example China is sponsoring the use of the SDR inside the World Bank. This will be something like the ECU in the term to be a basket or a virtual currency.

The financial NSA´s are full of brilliant minds and have an incredible power inside the markets but no one seems to have the fantasy to imagine a new currency. A currency backed by serious institutions.

What is the problem here?

Is it a lack of fantasy, of power or of ...credibility?

To be clear after Parmalat & 15/11 who will trust that

"currency" instead of the US dollar (and this despite the US stratospheric deficits)?

As we see it will be "easy"… it is only a matter of political wish.

But this does not happen, why?

In the next article we try to find an answer.

Notes   :
(I)   http://prosumerzen.net/2011/04/20/multinationals-as-no-state-actors-multinazionali-come-no-state-actors-derss/
(II)   http://prosumerzen.net/category/tarsga-%c2%a9-the-sustainable-risk-management/no-state-actors-nsa/
(III)   http://prosumerzen.net/2011/05/03/swf-world-info-monitor/
(IV)   http://prosumerzen.net/2011/05/10/sovereign-wealth-funds-weekly-monitor/

(Form of NSA: Private Financial Controllers, Functional Organizations,

Supervising International Organizations, Transnational Organized Crime,

Regional Organizations, Private International Powerhouse)

Chap. 36 - The new chapter of the war between No State Actors and State Actors: the currency war (2)

June 6, 2011

In the first part of this article, (I), we have introduced the new episode of the war between the Stare Actors, (SA), and some No State Actors, (NSA). We have told that the battle field could be a currency war and the 1st signal of it was the S&P´s, (an NSA in the category of Private Controller /PC, (II)), downgrade of the US bond. We have also told that it will be technically "easy" to try to reduce the role of the dollar if only there is a real political wish.

At least three actors can work, (also together); to achieve it but it seems that not one wants it. And this because all three despite their rhetoric and the credit of a power that is more supposed than real have neither the interest to do it nor the credibility, (power), to achieve it.

Who are the three actors?

1) The oil producers with political ambitions: Russia, Venezuela, Iran, (RIV)

2) China

3) Some NSA´s

They can work together and we have yet an "institutionalized" international arena, (an NSA that we can describe as Functional Organization/FO),and this is the SWF International Forum. The Beijing Communiqué´, (a logic evolution of the Santiago Principles, (III), issued on 12th May 2011 confirms it.

But, at least for the next time, it seems that this "alliance" cannot be realized.

Why?
Simply no one of them has interest to change the so-called "liberal American international order". They have interest on growing their role and power inside it not to substitute it. Also because they are well aware that even together they have neither the credibility nor the power to achieve that.

II – How the three actors could reduce the role of the dollar and increase the power of some NSA´s allied with some SA´s? And the problems they will face if they do it.
II. A – The stronger among them seems to be China.

How can Beijing achieve it?

China has almost six ways to achieve it, at least on theory.

1)Import/Export

Instead to use dollars to sell/buy Beijing can start to use the yuan. Doing that the market will be forced to take in account this currency and to ask for yuan instead of dollars. But doing that China will face incredible either international or internal problems. We must remember a key element of the Chinese development: China was and is, (even if less and less), the "inflation killer" of the world. Its reduced production costs were able to supply the required margin to the sellers keeping, at the same time, the inflation at bay. In the last years China is progressively losing this asset becoming more and more expansive to produce there and this is the natural evolution that Beijing has to face in order to maintain the internal stability. In other terms it happens that the Chinese workers "simply" want a better life and that the Government must develop a social net, (welfare), if it wants to preserve the political stability. About the Chinese key role as "world inflation killer" keep in mind that the average American family can save around 2.000 USD, (and the EU, South American or Japanese one not less that this amount),because can buy Made in China products and/or locally made products that use an high amount of Chinese semi manufactured components.

Now let´s imagine that Beijing asks to its national industrial champion, (NIC´s that in China they are less an NSA than in other countries), to buy/sell in yuan. Let´s imagine that, for example, Lenovo, (the biggest world OEM producer of computer with clients like HP), asks for it. This immediately will set the standard for all the computers and consumer electronics producers and will affect the prices for the worldwide buyers. The yuan will evaluate and the products will be more expansive. In other term China will start to export also INFLATION and Made in China products will be less competitive. If they will be less competitive China will sell less, (we have yet alternatives like Bangladesh, Vietnam, Laos, Cambodia, India and Africa), and this will create unemployment. With unemployment will rise the social tensions, (in 2010 the Government had to face not less than 100.000 manifestations), and this will be an unacceptable cost for the Communist Party that endorses the social stability, (and related preservation of the status quo), as its main strategic priority.

To be extremely clear we can synthesize all as follow: export accounts for the 40% of the Chinese GDP and that to the USA for its 25%. It means that the 40% of each point of growth is due to export and the 25% of it to the export to the USA. In other word for each generated renminbi 40 cents come from export and among them 25 cents thank to the American consumers.

Now the only strategic question is: can find China an alternative to the USA? Someone able to generate 25% of its GDP (or 25 cents for each generated renminbi if you prefer)?

The answer is simply NOT! (To be clear in the 2010 the biggest BRICS market for China was India, ranked as its world 7th, and no other BRICS was in the top 10. India import was 1/ 10 of that of Washington. In other terms if the American consumers generate the 25% of the Chinese GDP the BRICS ones generate around the 2% ...)

2) Oil and gas as well as other commodities starting with these from Africa.

Beijing can work with its allies like Russia, Iran and Venezuela to change the payment of oil and gas from dollar to yuan or to a new currency based on a basket dollar/yuan/euro. This will create a new standard and other can joint it. For example Brazil and India, (both BRICS), can start to sell oil/gas/bio-fuel, (Brazil), and to buy Iranian oil, (India), using this basket. But not only that. China is also one of the biggest world importers of other commodities, (copper, crop ...), and its biggest suppliers are in South America, Oceania, and Africa.

This will create a precedent.

The African countries consider Beijing as an economic partner used to make business avoiding to question about human rights, political freedom and so on. In other words to respect what they consider their sovereignty avoiding to interfere on it questioning about civil rights or rule of law. One of the lasting consequences of the Libyan war will be to see this role challenged from inside the network of the African political power. As we wrote,(IV),Gadhafi is a powerhouse in Africa and to understand it we can think to institutions like the Community of Sahel-Saharan States, (CEN-SAD), or the Common Market for Eastern and Southern Africa ,(COMESA),or the actions for a common financial market . The Libyan SWF has a particularly strong impact in Africa. There, the Libyan Arab African Investment Company had invested in over 25 countries, 22 of them in sub-Saharan Africa, and was planning to increase the investments over the next five years, especially in mining, manufacturing, tourism and telecommunications. Some examples of the importance of the Libyan investments:

- They have been crucial in the implementation of the first telecommunications satellite Ransom (Regional African Satellite Communications Organization), which entered into orbit in August 2010, allowing African countries to begin to become independent from the U.S. and European satellite networks, with an annual savings of hundreds of millions of dollars.

- Even more important were the Libyan investment in the implementation of three financial institutions launched by the African Union: the African Investment Bank,(AIB), based in

Tripoli, the African Monetary Fund,(AMF), based in Yaoundé (Cameroon), the African Central Bank, (ACB),with Based in Abuja (Nigeria). The development of these bodies would enable African countries to escape the control of the World Bank and International Monetary Fund and would mark the end of the CFA franc, the currency that 14 former French colonies are forced to use. Freezing Libyan funds deals a strong blow to the entire project.

But this is temporary and once Libya will find a solution in the next months the new government will back to play an important role in Africa that will affect the Chinese expansion in Africa.

Someone is wondering if the future government will have the skill to handle it. We think that they have the know-how simply because most of the seniors were seniors with the regime and defected at the begging of the revolution. These officers will use their know-how and connections as seniors of the new government and this government could be better work inside the international community as a responsible stake holder and as an allied of the EU and the USA. In this contest China will face a stronger competitive force. This because this approach is long-term based like the Chinese one and for this reason the best to compete with China because :" Beijing appears to have simultaneously cast the region as :

-a source for needed natural resources

-the next location for outsourced production,(our note : the next location for outsourced production CHEAPER than in China that is suffering for increasing labor costs since years and will soon face a decline of competitiveness)
-and a market for goods produced in China and by locally

based joint ventures
The underlying business focus is critical, because it suggests that while China is staunchly avoiding the sorts of conditionality seen in western development programming under the guise of respecting sovereignty,

The imperative that ventures be self-sustaining and profitable pushes evolution of the underlying governance structures that have emerged as the focus of development discourse. The reader is eventually left with the impression that a patient approach to the evolution of these structures combines with an emphasis on the physical infrastructure that forms the backbone of a developed economy to suggest that China has decided to invest and stay in Africa, not take a place as simply another development donor." (See Professor Burges on Professor Braütigam, V)

The impact of the Libyan SWF will reduce the Beijing 's political power to ask to these countries to get paid with an alternative currency as well as to pay ,(Made in China), using it.

1) Rare hearth materials

We have a product that has an incredible added value and where

Beijing controls not less than 85-90% of the world production. It is a mix of minerals generically described as rare heart materials.

They are not comparable in term of volume with oil or crop but they are controlled by China and here Beijing could start to ask, (using its monopole), to be paid in yuan.
Even if the global amount will be insignificant inside the

world mineral market it will have a strong political impact and it will be the "precedent" others can use for starting a shift away from the dollar.
It could... but it cannot, why?

Simply for two reasons:

I) Also in this case, as told at point B, this will generate inflation that will reduce the economic growth affecting the internal stability of the Country and this is unacceptable for the Chinese leadership

II) Beijing has lost the control of around the 50% of its export of rare hearth materials due to the smuggling by the local organized crime/OC, (at this point acting as an NSA), (VI), and they will sell in dollar.

4) The BRICS, (plus TIV = Turkey, Iran, Venezuela)

As told before China can orchestrate a BRICS Basket and the members can force their suppliers and clients to use it.

Additionally they can integrate the TIV, (Turkey, Iran, Venezuela), to create a common area for an alternative currency. And, logically, to persuade their allies to do the same using that "BRICS Basket".

Doing that Beijing can use an additional powerful tool of its International Economic Power, (IEP). This tool is its SWF and those of other BRICS, (for example Russia), or allied, (Iran), to be used as National International Economic Powerhouse / NIEP, (another kind of NSA).

But again the only effect will be inflation and an economic crash down that Beijing cannot afford to pay.

2) The SWF
Acting with the SWF Beijing can achieve a "multiplication effect" involving markets and private actors, (companies).

This is possible in, at least, three ways.

The 1st is to ask to the companies where they invested to start to use also this new currency and not only when they buy/sell to BRICS+TIV countries.

The 2nd is to ask to start to issue bonds using this mew currency and doing it supporting the creation of a market for financial product issued on that new currency. The third way is to use the political power of the companies where they have invested, (most of them are themselves NSA´s as Multinationals /MNC), and this in three ways

:
I) Asking to suppliers/buyers to use this new currency

II) Lobbying to their governments

III) Using their power, (either as stakeholders and as buyer of advertising),to "persuade" the media, (few of them are also NSA that we can describe as Global Media Outlets/GMO), to be benign with this new currency. And doing it they create the right "expectations" to increase its value, (or better, supposed value), more than its real weight inside the international markets. A clear example is about the bonds in renminbi issued by companies like McDonald and Caterpillar. For example Financial Times Deutschland makes a wrong calculation attributing a value of the 6% of the world financial market when it was the 0.06% (600 million renminbi are not the 6% of a market of more than 3 trillion dollars but Financial Times Deutschland wrote it in its 1st page). And doing that did not considered five "political" elements of the emissions:

I)The emissions were not issued in Shanghai = read it as a signal that the Chinese financial market is not yet ready to issue in its own currency

II) The emissions were issued by Western Banks = read it as a signal that no Chinese bank has the know-how to issue in its own currency

III) The amount,(for example 200 million of renminbi for McDonald),not only was insignificant at global level but it was that necessary to pay local operative costs A sound financial management suggests to multinationals to have local currency to pay local workers and suppliers, (from euro to yen …),and to use dollars when the local economy prefers it ,(dollarization).

IV) Not a lot followed the Western multinationals, (to confirm point C) = read it as a real evidence of the international wish to shift to a new currency…

V) It was NOT a Chinese multinational to do it and no Chinese multinationals are doing it = read it as an evidence that even Chinese companies have not interest to use its own national currency

All these elements were simply not mentioned in the general "clamor" about the issuing of bonds using the Chinese currency and this was not good because if they were and are considered we have the real image of the real impact of this event.

But this does not happen, why?

We must put all in the right contest and the right contest to understand the SWF is the Beijing Communiqué´ issued by the International Forum of the SWF´s as the logic evolution of the Santiago Principles.

The SWF´s are de facto NSA´s, (we can describe them as an Internal International Economic Powerhouse (IIEP), inside the international economic power of a country. They are engaged in a sort of "brand image building" because they want to avoid to be seen as "intruders" or as a" political tool of a third country". Doing that they are acting as NSA´s owned by State Actors, (SA), using an NSA like the IMF, (classified as International Organization), and, sometime, acting as investors in other NSA´s (Multinationals /MNC and National Industrial Champions/NIC).

An extremely complex situation, (as the Libyan SWF shows, VII), and Beijing as the owner of the biggest SWF in the world has not political interest to use it to start a currency war.

6) The Special Drawing Rights, (SDR).

The SDR are a virtual currency used only by the WB. Countries can have the right to draw this unit to face problems or to use for their reserves and must pay it with a real currency, (mostly doing it in US dollar).

This currency does not exists outside this circuit and has not a market, (and a value), for private entities like companies or citizens.

About the SDR as a tool to add a new world currency is interesting to read the brilliant proposal for a reform of the international monetary order by the Governor of the Central Bank of China Zhou Xiao chuan, (2009).

We do not mention about the problems to create a cost effective market for financial instruments issued with the SDR because they are like those of the ECU.

We focus on the "political problem "of the application of the reform. Beijing can use most of its reserves in US$ to buy SDR and ,maybe, the most interesting solution is that of using a "substitution account " as told by the General Director of Banca d'Italia Fabrizio Saccomanni , (1968 , 2010). That means that around 2 trillions of dollars will be invested on it. The only practical consequence will be to make the dollar even stronger, at least under a political dimension. Why? If the SDR are sold against dollar, (in a way that does not create turbulence in the markets), this simply means that the dollar itself is the "last warranty" able to cover the SDR´s. And again the USA that in this case are not only the country that prints the money used for its debt, (to quote President De Gaulle),but ALSO the country that prints the currency that will be used as "last resort" for the new world currency ,(the SDR´s).

On clear words the FED will be the real bank of the world or, better, the real co-bank if you prefer.

Something Beijing simply cannot accept....

Notes

(I) http://prosumerzen.net/2011/05/10/nsa-vs-sa-rumors-of-a-new-episode-of-their-war-this-time-inside-the-financial-market-1/

(II)   http://prosumerzen.net/2011/05/05/nsa-is-it-correct-the-description-of-the-21-kinds-of-nsa%c2%b4s-2/

(III)   The   Santiago   Principles http://prosumerzen.net/2011/05/13/swf-and-the-santiago-principles/
The   Beijing Comunique´http://prosumerzen.net/2011/05/13/official-comunicate-of-the-international-forum-of-swf-beijing-comunique%c2%b411-12511/

(IV)   http://prosumerzen.net/2011/05/03/swf-world-info-monitor/

(V) http://prosumerzen.net/2010/12/30/smugling-in-china/

(VI)   http://prosumerzen.net/2011/05/18/tactical-warning-libya-opec-swf/

(Form of NSA: Private Financial Controllers, Functional Organizations,

Supervising International Organizations, Transnational Organized Crime,

Regional Organizations, Private International Powerhouse)

Chap. 37 - Geo-political actors: the SWF an asset more for the SA against the NSA

March 6, 2011

It is interesting to remember one thing before that we start to evaluate the Sovereign Wealth Funds , (SWF), and it is the Governments are the owners of the biggest oil companies in the world ,(the 13 biggest in the world measured by reserves controlling more than 75% of the global oil/gas reserves and production ,(I)). This shift of power is happened during the last twenty years. Oil …

But those companies , (oil producers = OP),are only one of the four pillars of the so called "state capitalism" and the other 3 are :

1) The State-owned enterprises, (SOE)
2) The Privately owned national champions , (PONC)
3) The Sovereign Wealth Funds, (SWF´s)

We can draw the following equation of power of a State Authority, (SA):

OP+SOE+PONC+SWF + Central Bank + Foreign Aid + FDI +Import + Export = International Economic Power, (IEP).

Starting with this scenario we can better understand the SWF and their financial power, and how they are, maybe, the most dynamic element of a Country's IEP.

They are the strongest answer to the Non State Actors, (NSA), described as Multinational Companies, (MNC), and their (growing) divergent and contrasting interests with their own Governments, (III).

They can control them, (investing on them), influence them, (investing on Clients, Partners and Suppliers and affecting their relation with them), affect their reputation,(with the influence/control as stakeholders of the media).

One day the SWF will evolve in some kind of quasi-NSA controlled by a Government and this will be an interesting example of the evolution of the nation state as it is born after the Peace of Westphalia.

Three examples among others:

a) 2001: Iraq invaded Kuwait but never controlled its health that was always controlled in London by the Kuwait Investment Authority,(KIA). Saddam Hussein found the treasure chest empty. The KIA was an agency for Foreign Direct Investments, (FDI), and not at all a SWF but the FID were also ante-litteram SWF and we can consider that this situation can repeat

b) for example in Libya if the country will split ,(IV)

c) ... In this case the legal solution will be the law of war in case of war and in case of strong tensions what the Secretary of State Hilary Clinton told during her campaign as candidate. In both cases an interesting evolution of the international law and, more, of the concept of sovereign nationality.

Inside this geo-political contest if you are interested on a global compression of the world equation of powers as well as if you are interested on investments it is wise to monitor them as skilled and high-professional players.

In both cases it is what we in Prosumerzen describe as: Anti-risk Global Approach, (ARGA).

Notes :

(I)   The private owned companies control 10% of world's oil production and 3% of reserves.

(II)

    (II) Ian Bremmer – 2009

(III) The last NIC report about the trend till 2025 clearly mention that from now and that time there will be some conflicts ,(also using the force), between the US Governments and the US MNC due to different interests. In the 2006 the US Navy Naval College started a study about the use of the force ,(till the physical elimination), against US Citizen and/or Companies involved with black-listed Governments , NSA, entities.

(IV) "2 Libyas" :
http://prosumerzen.wordpress.com/2011/03/03/2-libyas/

(Form of NSA: Private Financial Controllers, Functional Organizations,

Supervising International Organizations, Transnational Organized Crime,

Regional Organizations, Private International Powerhouse)

Chap. 38:China and Lloyds: when a SA meets a NSA by Paolo Dealberti

February 6, 2012

The Chinese international real power as well as real influence is based on the performance of a few selected NSA´s.

China can sign anywhere in the world contracts to have commodities but because the USA will master the S3LC, (space, skies, sea, land, cyber),till 2070 Beijing can receive the mentioned commodities thanks to a benevolent Washington ,(clear text : till the USA will not decide to block the ocean routes).

China can hold USA bonds but it is the US economy that is back on tracks and three years of massive internal investments in order to create an internal demand have not been replaced the consumers in a mall in Minnesota or in California as main source of the Chinese growth . In other terms China buys bonds to buy markets and ,additionally, the menace to sell them is that of a "paper tiger" because no one will support Beijing on the destruction of the biggest economy of the world, (and not mention the Hilary Clinton ´s solution when she was candidate as President...).

China can veto in New York but cannot send 1 unit to help Assad.

Last but not least :

USA Import (2010) : 382.954 Mil USD

BRIS,(Brazil, Russia, India, South Africa),Import (2010): in the top 11 world markets for China we find only India and Russia = 40.914+29.612=70.529 Mil USD

In other terms if Beijing wants a war and to renounce to the US market must "only" find other 9,36 India or 12.93 Russia.

Something impossible at least in this planet and these numbers describe how the BRICS are more a "supposed " alternative consensus and new world order than a real one. By the way we kindly remind that in 2011 we had around 280.000 riots in China and that "simply" means that if Beijing cannot export enough to reach not less than a + 9% GDP/Y we have a dramatic social unrest if not a revolution. The geopolitical reason that forces Beijing to buy US deficit, (as well as Eurozone deficit),in order to buy shares of the US consumers is that there is not an alternative to the USA,(I),(as well as not to the EU).

The mentioned few selected NSA can be described ,(II), as :

- National Industrial Champions ,(NIC)

- National International Economic Powerhouse, (NIEP),and in this case we talk about the SWF.

- The Organized Crime ,(OC),because we suspect an organic structure like that in Russia .

For the moment we focus our attention on the NIC´s and the NIEP´s and under this light an event highlighted by the

Office of the President of the P.R. of China ,(III), offers an interesting example of the interactions between SA´s and NSA´s.

Inside the ceremonies for the to celebrate the centenary anniversary of the establishment of the Bank of China ,(BOC), and the forum for global systemically important banks the only photo is that with the Lloyds´ CEO. It is extremely symbolic because this meeting was used to talk about the international financial system reform and the healthy development of the global financial industry.

We at Prosumerzen are not surprised about this choice, (Lloyds). We consider Lloyds inside one of our editorial section, (Windhandel),because an NSA , (Private International Financial Powerhouse, PIFP, IV),and we have selected 7 on world basis thanks to the " NSA-SA Overlapping Index",(V), based on more then 400 variables evaluating the whole spectrum of the power from soft to hard power.

It is surely something extremely symbolic that we can describe as a perception generating perceptual implications.

Perceptual implications that are important because we human beings have an experience of the reality through our perceptions. In other term this perception is creating value and we can consider it inside the dimension of the soft power.

Notes:

I) http://prosumerzen.net/2012/02/03/the-mandarins-bain-company-the-next-billion-consumers/
II)Paolo Dealberti classificaion of 24 forms of NSA´s
III)http://prosumerzen.net/2012/02/06/presidential-desk-

china-lloyds-banking-group-plc/
IV) ibidem II
V) Paolo Dealberti

(Form of NSA: Holistic Powers, Global Media Outlets, Private Security Forces)

Chap.39 - Wikileaks and Stratfor: cui prodest

February 29, 2012

Let's imagine that the intelligence service of a Country informed the Parliament with ,let me say, not correct information about the risk of WMD and this to support the wish of the executive power. Then this service lost its credibility ... worldwide.

Then ,one day, someone with a multimillion dollar server infrastructure in a cave like a new Aladin finds the treasury and share it with us. Since that day the below mentioned intelligence service is again credible.

Credible about the incompetence of the President of Bavaria Mr. Seehofer ,(and President of the Sister Party that supports Chancellor Merkel), when international politics is at stake or about the bed used by Mr.Berlusconi for his bungabunga and son on.

And if you carefully analyze the sources of the information you find that the people in the cave used more dispatches from the secretariat of the Italian Socialist Party than from NATO ... of course classified information. It is amazing to know that the Secretary of the defunct Italian Socialist Party was able to supply more classified documents than the whole NATO!

It is not a movie it is Wikileaks and the CIA... and for internal as well as instrumental reasons too many have found these dispatches credible for the internal political struggle.

The result ? The CIA was again credible.. .

But ...one moment please ... **how does it with the mythology of the CIA-Mossad plot against Wikileaks fit ?**

Now let´s imagine a revolution and a dictators that sent tanks against his people and the last thing that the not armed civil on the street need is that someone, a credible source of information, blame them to be "puppet paid by the CIA".
According to Press TV that was told by Wikileaks ,(quoting another classified document), on April 2011 about the people on the street in Syria against Assad,(I).

Now it is time for Stratfor.

Sratfor is a NSA , (a *Private Intelligence Controller* , II),and belongs to an elite that lists the top advanced and sophisticated NSA´s in the last evolution of the Post-Westphalian order. An order where SA´s and NSA´s coexist and they coexist long before Westphalia.

It was easy to prove the Mr Putin gifted Mr Berlusconi of a bed but till today i is not proved if the last used it for bungabunga ... and so on. It is sad but ,till now,the information that we received form Wikileaks are a collection of data that any informed readers of two or three international newspapers or magazines yet know.

To be clear : its value is simply over-estimated by someone interested on it.

Nothing more and noting less even if we tend to forget it. On clear text : Wikileaks legitimized again the CIA ,(*at least about Mr Berlusconi´s bed*...), offering low level information and not a secret and what are we talking about?

The question is only and only one : cui prodest ?

Logically now and inside the confrontation NSA vs. SA.

Here is the key to find the answer.

Notes :

I)   http://prosumerzen.net/2011/04/18/president-assad-thanks-wikileaks/

II) Paolo Dealberti " Classification of the 24 forms of NSA´s"

(Form of NSA: International Consulting Company)

Chap. 40-The Mandarins : the Not State Actor N. 24

January 30, 2012

Paris 5th July 2011 a revolution started.

During a seminary the managing director of the leading French Think Tank Fondapol, Dominique Reynie´, announced a program for a revolution : to eliminate the Public Officer.

The Public Officer means the bureaucracy that is it the real "**4th power**",(after the legislative, executive and judiciary),as Sun Yatsen told at the beginning of the XX after 22 centuries of bureaucracy in China. He was ,among other, a master ,or better, a political teacher for Mao Dse Dong and Chang Kai-shek.

Weber told that the elected, (as member of the politically elected elite),has not a lot of power in front of the high bureaucrat because the last is in that department before of the first and the bureaucrat will be there after the elected. In other terms: the bureaucrat lasts and the elected changes.

The members of the **Politically Elected Elites,(PEE)**, are too busy to survive the daily struggles in the Parliaments and to focus on the next electoral term, (on average one each 8-12 months),to have time to think and for that they turn on Think Tanks. This is valid either for a President or for a Premier as well as for a MP.

But the PEE´s have an internal resource of "last resort" that is the bureaucracy that can contrast or ,at least, mitigate , the influences of the 6.545 Think Tanks in the world as well as of the ten , hundreds of thousands of lobbyists .

But if the Bureaucracy ,(the 4th power), will be scaled down ,who will replace this power ?

The International Consulting Company are suited to this role and to be the new Mandarins . With "Mandarins" we mean an high-skilled and ethically responsible elite as in the Confucian vision.

They are a small ,high skilled group of 11 companies .(in alphabetic order):

Accenture
Bain & Company
Booz & Company
(The) Boston Consulting Group
Deloitte Consulting
Ernst & Young
McKinsey & Company
Mercer LLC
Monitor Group
Oliver Wyman
PricewaterhouseCoopers

If this revolution will take place these Companies will replace the highest level of the Bureaucracy and because of that they will fit a vacuum of power between the Post Westphalia State Actors and the their society.

For this reason we consider them as the 24th category of NSA and we describe them as the **INTERNATIONAL ALTERNATIVE BUREAUCRACY ,(IAB)**.

The IAB's due to their deep relations also with the private economy will be a key element for the creation of new solutions" between a public sector that is on retreat since a generation due to the deficits and a private one that is finding ways to fill the vacuum in the society. The IAB´s will "bridge" this relation even if the Think Tanks as Influential Advising Entities ,(IAE,)will have the dominant role.

Complementary for the EEP´s will be the companies able to monitor the electorate , (pools), and the Rating Agencies that we consider an NSA described as "Private Controllers",(see our section about "The 16").

But we are also aware that something is changing and we consider six signals among others :

- the declaration about a back to something like the " Bank Act 1933" as part of the program of the Socialist candidate to the Presidential election in France François Hollande

- the deep geopolitical ,(but unlucky almost unnoticed), meaning of the Dagong Global Rating Co. ´s rating of Austria .(I)

- the revolution on 13-1-2012 with the S&P and Moody s ´rating on France. We can consider it as the confirmation inside this crisis of a nine centuries long trend that has been creating the Financial Real Economy ,(an economy parallel to the Industrial Real Economy)

- Chancelor Merkel´s failure to involve the banks in the EU Stability Fund

- that the EEP´s have placed the middle class at the core of their electoral programs, (for example see also the French Presidential candidate François Bayrou ,(II), as well as Obama that you can also monitor inside our "Presidential Desk" each Wednesday)

- the Indignados that represent a worldwide reaction stronger and deeper of the No Global movements and that from Tunisia is spreading all over the world assuming a local voice and character from the Arab Springs in Syria or Qatar to the "Occupy Wall Street Movements" This week we test "The Mandarins" to offer a carefully filtered selection of what is " the pulse of the world" for the IAB´s.

Other signals are developing and we will analyze them inside our editorials and tactical warnings.

Next week we will start to publish it each Friday.

Note :

(I) http://prosumerzen.net/2012/01/24/the-16-sisters-dagong-global-rating-co-rating-of-sudanaustriatrends-global-world-risk-outlook/

(II) http://www.fondapol.org/wp-content/uploads/2012/01/Intentions-de-vote-vague-3.pdf

(Form of NSA: Multinationals, NGO)

Chap. 41 - Bio-fuel can kill opium, cocaine, marijuana

March 31, 2011

If we consider the drug problem from the perspective of the farmers it is not a problem but, in most cases if not in all, the only way to survive.

This situation explains also the failure of most of the effort to convince them to convert their productions. The problem was and is: an international agency, an NGO partner of the local Government approach the farmers to offer money and know-how to convert to a different production. Then?

The next year prices fall down for a lot of reasons and/or funds are cut off, result?

Farmers need to feed their family and back to produce opium, marijuana or cocaine.

Sad but this is the real world but now we can offer an alternative **and a real, long term as well as sustainable solution.**

It name is bio-fuel and that means to produce corn and sugar to have bio-gasoline and bio-diesel.

France and Brasil can play a leading role.

How?

Brasil can offer the know-how to produce this fuel and France the market.

Both can support programs in Central and Latin America where farmers can produce corn and sugar that will be used for cars.

How can it work?

Player 1: Brasil

The country since 1975 is the front runner in the world production and today with 16.000.000.000 liters of bio-fuel pro year is the 2nd world largest producer after the USA.

Brasilia ,thanks to its extraordinary political power in Central and South America can support, projects to help Governments engaged in programs of agricultural conversion, (from cocaine, marijuana to an alternative production).

Brasil will buy this corn and sugar to use it to produce bio-fuel for the EU.

Player 2: Andean Region and Central American Governments

The regions more affected by the production either of cocaine or marijuana can implement with local as well as international NGO´s and UN Programs projects to produce corn and sugars to send to Brasil to be refined.

Or, as alternative, Brazilian companies can build up regional transformation plants and then export the bio-fuel.

Player 3: France

Paris has a long tradition in Brazil and its automotive industry is at the hedge in term of motors able to use bio-fuel.

Some data to confirm it.

a) Renault

In Brazil since 1997, (Ayton Senna industrial complex in Curitibia), and since 2008 has in Sao Paulo the Renault Design America, its first design center on the American continent. The center houses ten automotive design experts of Brazilian, Argentinean, Colombian and French nationality.

For example Sandero is one of the "full in Brazil" new international products.

Launched with an extraordinary success in December 2007 in Brazil and February 2008 in Argentina. Since 2009, is produced and sold in South Africa.

Renault has in Brazil a production of 118,209 vehicles, (=4.6% of the Group total), and a workforce: 4, 526, (= 3.5% of the Group).

b) PSA

Among others we magnify the 10th anniversary of the signature of an agreement for the Peugeot-ONF forestry carbon sink in Amazonia to be turned into a Private Natural Heritage Reserve (RPPN).

10 years to achieve the following success as be summed up:

- 2,000,000 trees reintroduced onto 1,800 hectares of former grasslands.

- 7,000 hectares of natural forest preserved and 1,200 hectares of Capoeira (natural recruit).

- Biodiversity restoration program, with over fifty native species reintroduced (a world first).

- 111,000 tons of CO2 sequestered in the biomass to date

- 2,300 pupils following the environmental education program welcomed onto the project between 2001 and 2008.

- Over 150 higher education students welcomed onto the project for multidisciplinary research

10 years is a long time in a world where Multinationals are used to think in term of quarters and this is a clear evidence of "green commitment".

France has the technology but also the market.

Paris can be the front runner in an initiative that can change the course of the history of the bio-fuel.

How?

The main problem to spread the utilization of the bio-fuel is that the current network of gasoline stations has not the hardware. And to add new pumps is a huge investment if it is not clear the trend of the market, (= how many drivers will ask for bio-fuel instead of the traditional one).

But Paris is one of the biggest buyer of cars and trucks in France, (if not the biggest), and this is for its police, army, bureaucracy.

Let's imagine that the Government tells that ,let me say, in 5 years from now all the cars that the government will buy will be …bio-fuel cars. And the first year it starts with the 30% of the total amount.

Then the government talks with the 2nd biggest buyer of cars: the rent car chains, (Hertz, Avis, Budget and so on). If they do the same they will have some fiscal benefit or subvention for each car, truck, (II).

Now we have the solution: the network of gas stations can forecast a reliable and sustainable market for bio-fuel and start to implement the hardware in the gas stations.

Logically as front runner Paris can promote this idea also at the EU level and also the EU farmers will benefit of this option.

We call it ...sustainable economy...

Notes

(I)http://www.peugeot.com/media/1030519/operation_carbon e_en.pdf

(II) The same for each company that will engage to substitute its fleet with bio-fuels cars and trucks.

(Form of NSA: Transnational Organized Crime)

Chap.42 -The Mexican drugs war as another scenario in the global war between Non State Actors and State Actors

June 3, 2011

Let´s imagine a Country where the Organized Crime, (OC), can act like a NSA, (No State Actor), and organizes its own military convoys. In this country an enemy cartel can organize its own military raid to intercept and destroy the convoy.

This land is not somewhere in some African or Central Asian turbulent region but it is a neighboring one of the USA.

We talk about Mexico.

It is not the first time that we mention about the "5 internal wars" in Mexico, (I), and how they are an interesting example of the NSA-dimension of the organized crimes or mafias. If we talk about not failed states it is a situation that we can find only in some regions in Italy, Germany, Turkey, Russia, Bulgaria, Serbia, Montenegro, Colombia, Kosovo, Macedonia, and Albania as well as in some provinces in China, Thailand, Brasil, Malaysia.

But nowhere the situation is so dramatic as in Mexico and we consider it as the most dangerous example of an **established parallel power inside a not failed state able to size and control territories within a state**.

The parallel power is that of the organized crime that is de facto a parallel state, (no state actor/NSA), and carrying the country to a civil war.

This happens few kilometers away San Diego or Laredo or El Paso and this magnifies and amplifies the strategic meaning of what is going on.
It sounds bit rhetoric to hear Washington to accuse Pakistan of being not able to seal its border with Afghanistan when it is not able to do that in Tijuana.
It sounds a bit rhetoric to hear the concern for the smuggling between Egypt and the Gaza Strip when the USA cannot stop the flow of weapons and money to Mexico and that of illegal immigrants, drug , criminals and potentially terrorists to its own territory.
It seems that the same lethal cocktail of BOTH side corruptions, interests, lack of resources and wrong done that we can find at the border between Egypt and the Gaza strip can be found at the border between California, Arizona, Texas and Mexico and we do not mention the illegal flow to Florida despite one of the most sophisticated and high tech trans-national system of surveillance in the world that the US Army and the NIA run in the region.
We respect the sacrifices and engagement of the US as well as Mexican officers but this does not change the situation that, for example, the US-run check-point in front of Tijuana is not less porous of any others at the border between Pakistan and Afghanistan.

Or that despite a multibillion dollars state of the art monitoring system, (from satellites to Echelon), plus, (at least since the beginning of the ′90s), local intelligence , covert operations and troops in the region a small Cessna without any electronic countermeasure can land into the American soil to smuggle anything from cocaine to terrorists. If the National Intelligence Agency, (NIA) cannot detect a small Cessna landing in the USA how can the most motivated and engaged Pakistani or Egyptian security officer,(that can only dream about that technology),find something smuggled in a truck ?

It is better as first to solve than to judge, accuse and advice and this **"simply" because it seems that we are all in the same boat and doing the same mistakes facing the same problems, is it?**

But this is not the problem that we want to analyze. We are interested on how the NSA´s are shaping the world. In a series of articles, (II), we are talking about the struggle between State Actors, (SA), and NSA inside the "financial front" and here we face a different dimension: the **control of the territory within a not failed state.**

Here we have all the ingredients of the cocktail:

> II) Strong and sophisticated drug cartels that are acting as an organized crime with the status of NSA
>
> III)
>
> II) An OC with control of the territory and a sophisticated military structure as well a "para-political" one able to gather consensus
>
> IV) This OC is deeply linked with other international OC and is the leading in the region, (at least till the Andean Region. We can consider Panama as the "borderline" of their influence)

V) A structure able to penetrate the neighbor state that ,by the way, happen to be the most powerful country in the world that since 10 years has invested billions of dollars to build up the most sophisticated defensive wall in the history of the humanity. And despite of that they can penetrate with less of 1 / 10000000000000000000 of the American technology and resources, (more than 2.3 trillion dollars invested in the last 14 years).

VI) Cartels deeply integrated in the international banking and financial systems thanks to hubs like Miami or the Gulf Islands ,(the last acting like offshore centers) VI) And with the money to pay the best legal advisers in the world in the USA

Lethal ingredients for an extremely dangerous cocktail that make the situation of these OC peculiar if compared with that of others like the Russian or the Italian one.

Again the main difference is that it happens few miles away the USA and it seems that 10 years of efforts to protect the American soil have not a lot of success on **stabilizing and protecting** its south flank.

We can consider one among the hundred acts of violence in Mexico, (that generated more than 25.000 deaths, or 3 each hour on average, in the 2010), as evidence of what we are telling.

May 27, 2001 Mexican Highway 15 near Ruiz, (Nayarit state) an armored convoy of 14 vehicles that belonged to the Los Zetas, (the most powerful cartel), were ambushed by members of the Sinaloa Federation. The Los Zeta lost the convoy, with the drug, money weapons that they were transporting as well as 29 of its members killed in the ambush.

We can describe it as a war operation involving armored vehicles, trained fighters, intelligence and high lethal weapons like RPGs. Something you can see in Iraq, Afghanistan but this time it was few hundred kilometers south of San Diego.

If we consider this action under a strict military point of view the evaluation suggests an alarming scenario:

A) Size is not enough.

We have groups able to fill an armored convoy of 14 vehicles and that mean not less than 56 skilled, heavy gunned criminals without reducing its operative power. And at the same time other groups are able to gather not less than other 80 or 100 criminals for an ambush and, at the same time, to be able to carry on their ordinary business without suffering any lack in term of operative capabilities.

B) Armored vehicles are not invulnerable

But not only such amount of gunned criminals but also with the operational skills and the sort of high-lethal weapons able to hit and destroy state of the art armored SUV vehicles.
If the point A tells us about a "quantitative" dimension of their

power what at point B informs us about the dangerous "qualitative" one.

C) Planning is all

Either the sending of a convoy by the Los Zetas inside an enemy territory then the ambush to stop it by the Sinaloa Federation are examples of "brain" more than of "muscles". On clear term it means to have intelligence capabilities and tactic as well as strategic skills.

Again something related with a structured parallel power and not with street gangs.

If we start from this military power and we put it in the right contest of an OC with a real control of the territory within a not failed state (and the 2nd US biggest export market as well as the 3rd world biggest supplier for the USA), like Mexico and we add to that the incredible international power, (both financial and military), they have we face the situation as it is. Or, if you prefer, the problem as it is. These cartels with their criminal links can reach Sao Paulo do Brasil, (the most sophisticated hacker hub in the Western hemisphere), as well as deliver drug in Berlin or Rome. Or super gangs that sell drug few hundred meters away the White House and that challenge the Washington Metropolitan Police for the control of the streets. But they can also invest money in legal businesses from San Diego to Tokyo. And also able to act as political catalyst supporting groups in a country involved in a war against its own government with the help of an external power, (for example the Colombian FNL allied with Venezuela against Colombia).

They are neither anymore only drug cartels nor a sophisticated organized crime structure because they are world class no state authors, (NSA),engaged ,(allied with other NSA´s), in a global as well as international war against the stare actors as originated by the post

Yalta order ,(the last evolution of the post-Westphalia order) , as started in the 1972 .

This is the real dimension of the "Great Game" in this corner of the world and Washington is not doing well.

An articulated structure that can offer safe heavens to any other NSAs, (III), and this:

- In a territory within a NOT failed state that is the 26th economy in the world.

- A state ,Mexico, that is the 2nd biggest world market for the Made in USA and the 3rd world biggest supplier for Washington ,(and about the strategic value of this import do not forget, for the example, the Mexican oil)

- Just in front of the border with the strongest country in the world and with trans-ethnical, (not only people with Mexican or Central /South American origins), deep roots all along this nation, (either legal than illegal).

And form this territory be able to do almost anything on world basis.
We wrote about the "5 wars" inside Mexico and this summarizes the geo-politic meaning of this situation under an international perspective.

The next big strategic problem for the USA, (and for the international security), will be this war against high sophisticated NSA´s harbored in places like Mexico, (the 26th economy in the world), more than something in Yemen or somewhere in Afghanistan.

To be clear such cartels are a lot more dangerous than Al Qaeda!

Notes   :
(I)   http://prosumerzen.net/2011/03/15/5-wars%e2%80%a6at-the-us-mexican-border/

(II)   http://prosumerzen.net/category/tarsga-%c2%a9-the-sustainable-risk-management/no-state-actors-nsa/

(III) http://prosumerzen.net/2011/05/05/nsa-is-it-correct-the-description-of-the-21-kinds-of-nsa%c2%b4s-2

(Form of NSA: Transnational organized crime)

Chap.43-The war against the organized crime: the revolution of the downsizing,(= selective targeting)

September 6, 2011

HOPE is the name of an anti-drug program run in Hawaii and now also in Alaska, Arizona, California and Washington. This program selects as targets the violent criminal drug addicts. It is about random controls and when someone is found using a drug is jailed and the probation or parole suspended. The result is impressive if we consider that 80% of the methamphetamine long-term users self clean-up after one year. Who is involved in HOPE is not forced to receive treatment instead they are required to stop to use drugs. Only 15% fails and it is forced to treatment. Since 2004, (the first application was in High Point, N. Carolina), is implemented by The National Network for Safe Communities the Drug Market Intervention Strategy. The strategy is to identify the most violent dealers in an area and to build cases against them. They are arrested and the message to other dealers is clear: if you avoid escalating to violent actions, to create crack-houses and to sell person-to-person in a street you will not in the selective targeting. Both strategies are downsizing the war against the drug focusing not on all the dealers or the users but, instead, only on the violent ones. It is more important to reduce the level of the violence and disorder in a community then to reduce the market.

Since years in places like Hawaii we assist to an evolution in the fight against the NSA described as Organized Crime. An NSA that controls around the 28% of the world GDP and it is the biggest and most lucrative industry in the world, (for example the Italian Mafia with more than 150 billion Euros revenue is the 8th biggest multinational in the world before Japan Post Holding and Chevron and a bit behind Toyota if it could be possible to rank Mafia Italia Holding in the Fortune 500 Top World Companies 2011).

Now this evolution could become a revolution sustained by heavy political and strategic analysis as well as academic works and an example is the brilliant article of Professor Mark Kleiman, ("Surgical strikes in the drug wars. Smarter policies for both sides of the border", Foreign Affairs Vol. 90 N.5 Sept/Oct 2011).

The basic elements of this vision focused on the situation between Mexico and the USA are the following:

- To focus on the interdiction of the traffics cannot solve the situation of the illicit drug market in the USA. This will simply change the routes of the traffic as the impressive aero-naval US power forced in the mid ´80´s the smugglers to abandon the Caribbean as export route to the USA and to start to use Mexico. This will achieve only to relocate to new routes the traffic but it will never affect the demand in the USA. The cost that has been asking to the Mexican people to achieve is, (around 1.000 deaths each month), it is too high. By the way from a strategic point of view is important to wonder where the new routes will be developed if it will not possible via Caribbean and Mexico. Could it be Canada via Europe? Or Alaska via Russia?

- The problems in term of violence and disorder are created by small minorities of hard users that are consuming around 80% of the illicit drugs

- To destroy the production of cannabis in the USA is creating a substitutive production in Mexico that are increasing the level of violence for something that is not consumed in the USA

- To increase the number of arrested dealers, (now around 500.000), will make worst the problem of the penitentiary system and not alleviate the situation in term of reduced violence. This because only a minority of the dealers are the trouble makers

- To legalize the use of illicit drugs is not a solution if we consider that around 50% of the detained persons in the USA committed a crime when drunk. To make easier to find drugs can only increase the problem. To think to a fiscal policy of high tax to reduce the legal utilization, (like with tobacco and alcohol), will only push the price to a level that will stimulate again an illegal market, (like with the smuggle of cigarettes)

- 40 years of war against the illicit drugs have demonstrated the failure of the classic mix of actions: enforcement, prevention, treatment, (EPT).

As we mentioned months ago talking about the five wars inside the Mexican war among gangs involved in the illicit drugs business,(I),we agree about the situation in Mexico. Mexico and the USA are facing what Kleiman describes as the great asymmetry. A situation where the drug problem is central in the USA and accidental in Mexico. This because the USA are the market, (the buyer), and Mexico the route of transit of a production mostly made in the Andean Region. If the USA does not demand the volume of drugs is demanding or if the routes were in the Caribbean, (as it was till the mid ´80´s), Mexico should have not this level of violence.

But about the rest we are interested on going ahead with the Kleiman´s suggestions and to evaluate why this is now a revolution more than an evolution in the strategy against the organized crime.

To do that with have to shortly evaluate the **40 years process of downsizing and shift of priorities and targets in the war against the crime**.

At the beginning it was seen and evaluated as a social problem. A group of people started to use illicit drugs and to become addicts. The reasons were found in the society and they were seen as victims. The strategy was to eradicate the reasons that in a society can drive someone to become a hard-user.

It was found that it was simply impossible to eradicate those reasons and the strategy downsized focusing on the stopping of the traffic and selling.

It was to declare a war against the groups that produced, traded and sold drugs. Maybe the most apparent effort in the world was that of the USA in the Caribbean and Andean region with a financial and military engagement. The destruction of the Medellin Cartel with the killing of Pablo Escobar and an invasion to arrest a drug smuggler like the former President of Panama Noriega are the most known examples.
But it seems that after more than a quarter of century also this strategy is failed. Statistics shows that after each clean-up made by the authorities a new group raise to substitute the producer, the traders and the dealers. And unlucky a recession will generate enough people motivated to find an easy to get money with an involvement inside this illegal market.

Now the downsizing finds an intellectual and academic support to reach a step forward: **the problem is not the traffic or the selling on itself but if it generates violence and social disorder.**

The solution is that of a selected targeting where the targets are:

- Only the violent hard-users
- Only the violent dealers
- Only the violent traffickers

For example Kleiman suggests that a way to achieve a sharp and fast reduction of the level of violence in Mexico is that to create metrics to rank the six leading cartels according their violence. Then to target in the USA the dealers that have them as suppliers. This is possible because the US anti-drug authorities claim to know who the supplier of each group of dealers is. Because the dealers will be a selected target because they buy from the most violent cartel they will change the supplier. In other words the law of market will force the cartels in Mexico to be less violent in order to avoid losing clients in the USA.

If we consider that this approach sounds we can extend it also to the producers, in other terms to target only the producers that transport using violent traffickers or sell to violent dealers.

Those producers to avoid to be targeted will refuse to sell to violent buyers and the buyers to avoid losing the suppliers will be less violent. But with the same logic violent producers will be a target and the buyers to avoid becoming itself a selected target will shift to less violent producers. All should initiate a virtuoso process of reduction of the general level of violence from Colombia to Afghanistan. This is the theory. Unlucky the USA did not apply this strategy in Afghanistan against the war lords that used opium to finance their power and it seems that Washington will never do it. It is not a matter of military power. To bombard the opium fields with herbicide in order to destroy the cultivations is something that the USA has the military power to do even if not an American soldier is in Afghanistan. Today the satellites inform about the location of the fields and in few days the USAF can destroy the production. But it seems that for Washington costs less to have the drug, (with the related social problems and costs in term of violence), in the American streets than to destroy the production of some war lords and, consequently, to lose their support. In other words it seems that to have violent dealers and hard-users that kill in the American street is not such a cost and danger for the National Security like the risk to lose the support of a war lord in southern Afghanistan.

This example can show how this strategy can collapse once it faces the reality of the international politics. And each country that produce drugs is, unlucky, a strategic player in any local exchequer, (as well as any transit country like Mexico or Albania or Turkey or Italy…).

Kleiman's approach is valid in some contests and in some situation and can be used and be extremely effective. Logically it has to be used together with the EPT approach but, as told, we are not here to talk about it.

We are here to evaluate how the further escalation of this downsizing toward less complex targets ,(from the change of what in society can be the source of the use of illicit drugs to the selective targeting of violent users and dealers), can originate a revolution in the relation between the states and the NSA called Organized Crime.

But before to go ahead it is interesting to remember four facts happened in Italy, Mexico, Peru 'and in some African Countries.

-Italy 1982, Rino Formica was a member of the Italian government and proposed an amnesty to the camorristi, (members of the camorra), if the leave the organization and also to buy the offshore boats they used to smuggle as a way to finance their integration in the legal way, (the money was supposed to be a capital an ex-camorrista should use to start a job).

-Mexico 2011 , the former foreign minister Jorge Castaneda proposed an amnesty for the cartels that want to suspend any illegal activity and to let them to invest their black money inside the legal economy.

-Due the economic consequences for an interesting part of the farmers on 18-8-2011 Peru has suspended the strategy of eradication of the opium fields.

-In July 2011 the Italian Divisione Investigativa Antimafia , (DIA , anti-mafia investigative unit),denounced that different criminal groups were involved on buying the title of Consul or Plenipotentiary Ambassador in country like Ghana, Nigeria, Senegal in order to hide their members behind the diplomatic immunity.

Those facts are, simply, telling us that it is not new to imagine a downsizing that can go well beyond the Kleinman´s approach and that can reach the borderline to offer to the Organized Crime the impunity or the immunity in order to reintegrate the black money inside the legal economy.

If Mafia Italia Holding ,(we use the term holding because the Italian mafia is composed by different mafias : mafia del Brenta in Veneto, n´drangheta in Calabria, camorra in Campania,sacra corona unita in Puglia, cosa nostra in Sicilia),is the 8th multinational in the world and for that bigger than Microsoft or Nestle that means something. And it means something also that around the 28% of the world GDP is originated by all the world mafias that are composing the NSA described as Organized Crime, (II).

What does it mean?

"Simply" ,(and unlucky),that the biggest holder of liquidity in the world is neither the Bank of China, nor the Chinese Sovereign World Funds or the SWF´s of the International Forum of the SWF but the Organized Crime Holding , (OCH).
If you want to see the situation in a different perspective the most stabilizing financial force in the world after the concerted action of the Central Banks are not some conservative pension funds that act against the speculation but the OCH that can use its tremendous financial power to stabilize a market.

And, consequently, the most destabilizing force in the financial markets is not the coalition of some speculative hedge funds but, again, OCH that can speculate without limit in term of money to invest.

We are living in markets where uncontrolled voices, (without a lot of real competence if we consider that all the rating firms told that Lehman was a superlative investment on 14-9-2008 and then the bank bankrupted on 15-9-2008....and not mention Parma at, Enron...), can support the laser focused action of a small group of speculators that are acting without the money to back their buy/sell but only using some financial instruments that give them this power. Let´s imagine now if a power with real money behind will use the same instruments with a buying power that is two or three magnitude bigger than that of the speculators.

In other term the real political problem against the division of Italy in two is the concern about the risk of the creation of a state with the euro, an integrated financial market and ... with the money of Mafia Holding and of Organized Crime

Holding that can flow without any control in the legal economy.

But if we consider this downsizing approach this will be the inevitable step in the next years in a world that needs money to re-start and to stabilize.

The next step will be: if you want to avoid to be a selected target you have to accept our conditions to finish any illegal activity and to put your money, (that we need), in the legal economy.

The only political point that that day will count is to see if the State Actors, as we know them from the order imposed by the Peace of Westphalia, will have the power to dictate the frame of the agreement instead to be forced to accept one from the NSA called Organized Crime Holding.

Notes

I) ttp://prosumerzen.net/2011/06/03/the-mexican-drugs-war-as-another-scenario-if-the-global-war-between-no-state-actors-and-state-actors/h

II) About the NSA´s and the download of a document about the existing 21 types of NSA´s at: http://prosumerzen.net/category/from-geopolitics-to-biopsherepolitics/no-state-actors-nsa/

(Form of NSA: Functional Organization)

Chap. 44 - Art .5, the risk of war between NATO and Syria

November 25, 2011

This morning we have published a Tactical Warning about the deployment of a US Navy nuclear carrier in front of the coasts of Syria.

Among others ,(I), it was wrote:

"Tactical Warning Military 1 : We do not think to an action at least in the next 7-10 days.

Tactical Warning Military 2 : but there is the option that some forces inside the regime want to drill this to weaken Assad ,(IV), and kill some Turkish as well as to make some raids inside Turkey against the refugee camp only to act as " agent provocateur" and force Assad to resign and shift the power to his brother. This will be made to try to increase the pressure creating some acceleration ,(due to the provocation), on what told at point 1 "

Thanks to the Art. 5 of the NATO if a member of the alliance is attacked the whole alliance reacts to defend. Turkey is a member of the alliance.

This morning the Turkish Foreign Minister stated that Syria is beyond any limit of tolerance due the brutal repression.

On may 6, 2001 ,(II),we have informed about strong struggles inside the leaderships of Iran and Syria.

Now we draw a possible scenario.

A strong Turkish retaliation , even without the risk of a NATO support but with the intelligence /counter-electronics help from the USA and Israel, will force changes either in :

- Syria
- Iran
- and inside the Iranian proxy clients Hezbollah and Hamas

We can think that factions against Assad and Ahmadinejad could forge an alliance. They can create some incidents with Turkey.

For example :

- to kill others Turkish citizens in Syria

- to attack the embassy in Damascus during a manifestation

- to penetrate in the Turkish territory to attack either the refugee and/or Turkish targets

The consequent pressure from Ankara will change the equilibrium inside the two regimes.

This could force Assad to shift the power to his norther and brother -in-law.

In Iran will weaken Ahmadinejad.

Consequently for the next months also Hezbollah and Hamas will be weaken because their supporter ,(Iran),and its proxy client , (Syria) , will be engulfed in the internal struggle.

We do not think that these provocations will cause a war between Turkey and Syria as retaliation and then, consequently, the NATO will be involved because of the Art. 5.

Turkey could retaliate and its military power can do it without fearing a Syrian reaction. **This retaliation will not involve**

the NATO but will be supported by the counter-electronics capabilities of the US Navy Ronald Reagan´s battle group as well as from these of Israel. Additionally the USA will supply intelligence thanks to satellites and echelon. The combined action of these counter-measures will blind the Syrian army and let the Turkish to implement a laser focused strike without any lost of pilots and /or commandos.

This military pressure will be used by the Assad and Ahmadinejad ´s internal enemies to remove the first and to weaken the last and in this case the next time will be to remove the Iranian Premier in the coming months.

Note

I)http://prosumerzen.net/2011/11/25/tactucal-warning-us-carrier-in-front-of-syria/

II)   http://prosumerzen.net/2011/05/06/tactical-warning-iran-and-syria/

(Form of NSA: Terrorism)

Chap.45-Post –Osama, better post- Al Qaida

June 24, 2011

I am in a lounge inside an international airport and I sit alone drinking a superlative coffee starting to realize that Bin Laden was hunted more than Adolf Hitler. When I come to this idea I get sad.

In the '80s there was an equivalent collective drama and the protagonist were Carlos the Jackal but his face was not so notorious like that of OBL. It was because a different era with less access to media, maybe....

OBL was found and among them who will benefit for this event we can account also the Pakistani intelligence that will see a sharp increase of the legend about its ability to deceive the whole world, including its own government.

Now it seems that the new leadership is not so strong...one moment please, so strong?

What did Al Qaeda achieved in 10 years? Nothing.

Maybe it is time to understand something we have been missing since years.

Al Qaeda is a group characterized by:

- crude unsophisticated rhetoric
- obnoxious behavior
- ugly sectarianism

- the tendency of its various "franchised" affiliates to alienate almost everybody
-a predilection to engage in vicious infighting

But not only this. Too many have used terabytes and ocean of ink to try to understand because this message of violence could have some appeal for the youths. A lot of theories raised and they talk about almost anything from the social evolution since the VII AC to how "rap Jihaidist"music can affect a fragile mind....

But we have not found an answer and, more important as well as more tragic, we have missed something.

What?

We missed the internal and lethal crisis of this movement that continued to receive support and gain adherents **despite of its ideology, and not because of it**. Inside our ivory towers of supposed knowledge about others we were so concentrated on talking about "how we can conquest hearts and minds" that we did not track something in the streets. And this something is that the majority of Muslims find its vicious sectarianism, callous narrow-mindedness and pedantic fixation with details at the expense of the whole picture, extremely infuriating, and often repulsive. The only, (residual), support come thank a powerful anti-Western rhetoric and to the legend of an over-estimated, (by the intelligence communities), operative power.

It is better to remember something: 1989. It was a moment of hope in the west. But unlucky we cannot tell the same for the Greater Middle East. And unlucky there was no shortage of people that wanted to fight for their (own) local wars. Hamas,

Hizbhullah, Kasminiris…and Al Qaeda.

Yes we have not to forget that at the origin AQ was a local enterprise run by OBL obsessed to driving the US Troops outside the KSA. By the way, we think that we have to put it also inside the internal struggles in the Kingdom and we are sure that, one day, someone will start to write also this missing chapter of the history. Then and only when he associated Adman Al-Zawahiri emerged within a group whose ideology distinctly called for targeting the "proximate enemy", (read the dictatorial regimes at home **rather than** Israel or America).

BUT with both failing, (to target the KSA elite and the dictatorial regimes in the region), they were forced in to exile. At this point to get sufficient support for their local wars they decided to make a virtue out of a necessity and declare war on America, the West and Israel.

And this is the key point that we always missed and are still missing. OBL &. Co. declared war to the USA/West/Israel NOT because they had success at home and were strong BUT because they have any success at home and they see that this could be the best marketing tool to promote themselves.

On clear words: OBL Saudi supporters shared the ideology of the monarchy, which enforced the structures of Wahhabi Islam. To ask them to a fight against an Islamic monarchy would have not been an easy order, but to direct their frustrations and ire against the "infidel Americans" who occupied the "Prophet's Peninsula" was an easier sell. Then the fight against the US/West started to be the best marketing tool they had also to try to re-direct the anger of the varied local insurgencies towards America, and thus secure global support for his local war. We shortly remember that AQ never attacked an Israeli target, (both in Israel or abroad), and this to confirm both how its military power was /is more supposed than real, (and at least a lot over estimated), and that Palestinians were never a reason to fight for OBL.

But also in this case the success was limited because:

-many groups refused to join the fight
- some withdrew after joining.
- When the group appeared to expand into some new regions, (Iraq, Yemen, North Africa), this was even more disastrous for it because the new adherents were the worst advertisement for any movement: brutal and brutish, maliciously sectarian and pathologically bloodthirsty, (at a such level that the achieved the sad score to provoke more revolts against them than against their enemies)

In a sentence: they demonstrated the bankruptcy of the terror route.

And if we want evidence look at the Jasmine Revolution: where is Al Qaeda?

When do we decide to enter in a post-Al Qaeda world?

(Form of NSA: Holistic Powers, Terrorism)

Chap.46 - 22/7: White Christian Fundamentalists, (WCF)

July 28, 2011

(Editorial Note : on May 2012 a Panel of 76 world class specialists run by the prestigious Foreign Policy confirmed what we told describing the menace generate by the WFC´s as the 3rd most dangerous for the USA)

1-Ideas = words with a dynamic meaning and an inner symbolism

Our life runs around a lot of complex and diversified ideas but, at the end of the day, we can describe them with relative few words. For example:

freedom,peace,war,rights,duties,membership,citizenship,law ,order,justice,respect,love,friendship,family,healt,wealth,pove rty,ecology,sustainability,politics,economy,security,style,cultu re,art,gender,discrimination,racism,woman,man,child,educati on

… We can think not more than around 100 words.

Not a lot and sometime, (in a historic slow process), we add new words that we invent to describe a ,(new), situation , for example :computer, revolution, bourgeoisie

, communism, fascism, nazism, socialism ,globalization, internet, social networks …
If that means something it is that we can describe each change of the world thanks to ideas that give a different meaning to ,(the same),words.

Different ideas expressed with the same words that have a (deep) different meaning. If words have this strength 7/22 will have the same value of 9/11 and it will be another of its consequences as also it is 9/15 as part of the war between State Actors and No State Actors, (I).If 9/11 was the codeword for 10 years of war against an external enemy 7/22 will be the codeword for a war against an internal enemy. And this war will be more painful and bloodiest of that originated with 9/11 "simply" because the enemies are among us and come from us. It will be a war against our self, against the black side of our societies. We can consider 9/11as the expression of a failed revolution and attempt to originate a civil war, (I), inside the Arabic Peninsula before than inside the Muslim World. When Bin Laden realized that he cannot initiate a civil war, a revolution inside the Arabic Peninsula for a lack of followers and because of the reaction of the local regime in the KSA .It is hard to believe that for 10 years we lived under a collective paranoia and that we were thinking that a network of terrorists that have problems to reach consensus even at home could be able to win the west and to establish a global Caliphate. Historians will have problems to understand how rational and skilled elites could believe that Bin Laden could achieve what Hitler, Mussolini, Imperial Japan or the USSR with an ideology with a real and global appeal for their contemporaries and an astonishing military power did not achieve. In any case the Jasmine Revolution has been showing and demonstrating that people are tired of fundamentalism.

But 9/11 had also a different meaning and this explains also because the war to win "hearts and mind" was never won.

9/11 was the first international revolution born outside the western culture since centuries.

From the American Revolution to communism or nazi-fascism each ideology that was able to shape the world and try to establish a universal order was "made in the west". We could use Plato, Aristotle, St.Agustin, Calvin, Rousseau, Franklin, Marx, Nietzsche, Hegel to explain all and to read the entire world and its future under a perspective born inside our culture and using our "genetic code" to decode and understand.

With 9/11 we introduce new words and ideas that not only were unknown for the most but also "alien" to us, (alien with the meaning that we have not the sensibility to understand and appreciate them,). The consequence was an arrogant race to appropriate these words, codes and ideas and to try to read them under our culture. We spent ocean of inks to discuss the Sutras that should justify the Jihad but how many of these writers read the Koran?

And so on...simply for the first time since centuries a movement was not born influenced by a western ideology, (for example like with communism), and using as reference our thinkers. We share a common heritage with Plato and Aristotle if, for example, Pico Della Mirandola was influenced by Averroes but that was useless to understand what behind and around 9/11.

It was a revolution born with a different genetic code and if it will have a legacy this legacy will be that it used different meanings for the seam words and a meaning that was totally unknown to us.

And this is the biggest and deeper difference between 9/11 and 7/22.

To understand the difference we have to focus on what 7/22 is similar and observing the images in Oslo we can remember Oklahoma City .Another nazi terror attack on 19-4-1995, (the biggest act of terrorism in the US history after 9/11).

The same Christian fundamentalism, the same target, and even the same bomb.

But if we talk about 4/19 we have not forget that it was not alone and that after that a long sequence of nazi – fundamentalist Christians terror attacks hit the USA. The last was 8-1-2011 in Tucson and the author motivated it as follow:" There is a vast left-wing conspiracy in this country and these liberals are working together to attack every decent & honorable institution in the nation."

Left-wing conspiracy? The attack that killed so many in innocents in Utoya was against a convention of young members of the Labor Party.

An attack to a symbol inside the symbol. The first symbol is that to attack a modern and tolerant political force and the second is to attack its future killing its youth members. This is the first evidence that we are talking about an act that is not isolated but with deep root inside an international network of Christian fundamentalists.

2- A surprise?

Not at all at least for Prosumerzen because since months we are telling that the next "big attack" will not be made by Jihadists but by Nazis WFC.

Unlucky there is nothing to be amazed. For ten years the center and far right parties have played with the fire of the fear against the social integration to justify the economic problems and to hide a lack of solutions and no one can be surprised that at a given moment the Pandora's box is opened with a massacre.

No one of these that sent a warning about an Europe full of Minarets could for a second trust their own words and to think that this could be a realistic scenario, Again Al Qaeda with around less than 1.000 fighters can conquest the west and the world when the USSR with around 35.000 nukes, 2 million soldiers, a rich country like Russia behind and allied all over the world failed…who can believe that? The fundamentalist evangelist priest that burned a copy of the Koran was giving a moral justification for any violence against the "foreigner", the "different" and against anyone supported them.

That was told and told and told for ten years and that generated a feeling of intolerance and fear that was supposed to be the solution. Now more than 60 tombs in Norway tell us that this never was a solution but only a problem.
It could lead to a temporary loss of popularity for the far right, but long-term repercussions for the far right are unlikely since these parties have begun tempering their platforms in order to attract a wider constituency and be part of the elected elite and establishment in order to see the application of their policies from within.

3-Alone?

If we consider the top 60 terror groups in the world around half of them are based on religion and all religions are involved.

It is strange but anytime we face a Christian fundamentalist attacks the perpetrators are alone. We wonder what happens if the attack were run by Jihadists. In less than 1 hour the world will be invaded by evidences and comments about a global network of terror able to finance, plan and execute it. But when is made by nazi WFC it is always something done by someone alone or by a small group without any link.

Is it a bit strange?

Someone can buy fertilizer but to create a bomb needs training and advising.

But look at the weapon used in Utoya. We are not talking about a machine gun but about a semi-automatic weapon, (a semiautomatic 5.56-caliber Ruger Mini-14 rifle and a 9 mm Glock pistol). Nothing, that only super terrorists can buy.

But the point is not to describe the dynamic of the attack but that it is strange that each time we face a nazi WFC all the world runs to tell that it is the act of someone alone and not part of a strategy by a group part of a global network with the aim to destroy our way of life and to substitute it with a neo-nazi dictatorship where if someone is "different", (color, religion, gay, lesbian, political belief), deserves only to be killed..

Why?

"Simply" because the WFC are part of us and they kill us and this can be described like a civil war. Civil war describes better than terrorism. An act of terrorism would attack a Muslim target in the EU or in the USA but if the WCF´s attack and kill Europeans in Europe, (the Norwegians are EU citizens), or American, (Californians or Minnesotans), in the USA we are talking about civil war.

The fear related to this word suggests to use the word terrorism and to talk about the action of a solitary attacker linked to small marginalized groups.

4) International WCF

What told at the end of the paragraph 3 introduces about the international WCF network and movements.

As told it is hard to find that it is talked about an international movements if we consider how it is easy to tell that each small act of political violence or terror by a Muslim is a well plan and coordinated part of a broader strategy that involves not less than some countries and "franchisee" of supposed and so-called super efficient terror groups. An explication can be found if we consider the following elements:

a) The WCF are linked to strong powers that are deep linked inside our societies. Political, economic, intellectual, holistic and religious powers and this explain the "concern" to talk about them, (some of them are also NSA´s).

b) They have not only supporters and followers but there is also a big "grey area", a sort of social vacuum, where a lot of normal citizens even if they have nothing to do and share with them can find, ("at least"), some reasons on what they tell. On clear term these citizens surely not agree with violent and indiscriminate acts against someone only because a foreigner or a Muslim but surely agree on the fact that one reason of the increased small criminality is due to the present of some foreigners and so on.

c) The WCF´s live and work in our societies and they are known as member of the community. It is hard to blame someone that you meet each day and surely it is easier to blame someone that you not know or does not belong to your social group or community.

This network includes:

- Violent anti-abortion activists
- Violent anti-lesbian and anti-gay activists
- Neo-nazi
- Violent far right groups
- Ultra nationalists also in countries like Russia or Serbia ,(orthodox and for that members of the Christian family of belief) or in
Turkey as well as in Lebanon and ultra-Zionists in Israel.
- Violent or extremist separatists for whom the "ethnic factor" is a matter of difference and an excuse for violence
- Christian fundamentalists religious groups
- Holistic groups linked to a fundamentalist vision of the Christianity, (NSA)
- Militia as these involved in 4/19

This is an international network of movements that interests different members of the Christian family of belief such evangelicals, protestants, Methodists, catholic, orthodox. A network that embodies also contrasting visions about the international politics and the best example is Israel. Some evangelical groups in the USA and in the UK are supporting the most extremist Zionist groups when the catholic are against Israel. This finds its roots on historical and cultural roots: for the Anglo-American we can find it on some interpretations of the myths about the "12 tribe" related to some visions of the Pilgrim Fathers and for the catholic we can find it on the same racist aptitude in Spain in XV.

This constellation of movements has a deep root in the societies of different countries and they reach two main social groups. And it is hard to believe that Breivik is alone because he is part of a larger organization that he calls the "Pauperes Commilitones Christi Templique Solomonici (PCCTS, also known as the Knights Templar), which seeks to encourage other lone wolves (whom Brevik refers to as "Justiciar Knights") and small cells in other parts of Europe to carry out a plan to "save" Europe and European culture from destruction.

5) Their social roots: **L Generation, Reducing Expectations Middle Class, World Middle Class**

The international Christian fundamentalism is deep rooted in two of the biggest and most sensitive social group in the world.

One is the **LOST GENERATION, (L Generation**, (III)), and the **WORLD MIDDLE CLASS, (WMC)**. About the WMC we consider the description by Homi Kharas, (III), and we can consider a transnational social group of around 1.9 billion people.
About the L Generation we consider the description in an article in Prosumerzen, (IV), and we can consider a social group of around 1.2 billion people.

The two groups are overlapping because ,(especially after 9/15),of the economic crisis and we can describe this trend adding a new transnational social group that we describe as **REDUCING EXPECTATIONS MIDDLE CLASS** , **(REMC)**,and we can consider around 400 million people. To better understand who belong to these groups we use Kharas´s parameters. According to the OECD Paper members of the WMC are people that can afford to spend each day between 10 and 100 USD. Starting from this value we can describe the other two groups as follow:

a) The L Generation is people that can afford to spend between 8 and 20 USD each day but with short term contracts or part-time job. In Germany are described as "poor even if with a job". But the most important element to characterize the L Generation is that they have not a future because their jobs do not offer them any chance to think to a retirement as well as to have the credit for an home, (for them it is a problem even to have a contract to rent a flat and this because they cannot offer the warranty of a job and this explains because they cannot afford to leave the family .But also a credit of 20€/monthly to buy a smart phone is a problem ! And this explains why the phone providers offer smart phones inside the monthly flat rate and without this solution we can be sure that we will see a lot less iPod or HTC or Blackberry).

b) The REMC are these among the WMC that have reduced their expectations either in term of living standard and about the future, (for example an house or the universities for their sons).We can consider among them a group of around 400 million people inside the world middle class.

An additional tragic element is that the so-called social mobility interests the L Generation that can move up to reach the lowest level of the WMC,(in the range of a purchasing power between 10 and 30 USD/daily) as well as the WMC and the REMC that can move down and become REMC or L Generation.

In a sentence: the feeling that there is not future and only a life of reduced expectations.

These people are educated and represent the most vibrant section of a society and it is not by coincidence that they also the voters that they less and less vote and the exceptions to this trend are a vote like the last referendum in Italy where the promoters where not the official and established political parties.

If we translate it on the European and US political landscape we can agree with Marko Panic, (V), and "The *attack in Norway has prompted a debate in Europe over whether the recent electoral success of far-right parties has had any causal linkages to the attack of extremism on full display in Oslo. Recent success of far-right parties across Europe has actually a lot to do with the fact that the extremist far right has cleaned up and become part of the mainstream. One of the main avenues of electoral success has been the idea that the far right, especially in Nordic and northern Europe — so countries such as Sweden, Finland, Denmark, the Netherlands — that the far right in these countries is actually the last bastion of liberalism and protector of European-styled tolerance. The idea being that the reason these parties are anti-immigrant is because immigrants coming to Europe, specifically Muslims are intolerant and that they therefore cannot be part of a tolerant, liberal society. This has played very well with voters in northern Europe. However, there could be a mechanical linkage between the legitimization of the far right on the electoral side of things and the rise of extremism such as what was on display in Norway. In particular, as the far right becomes part of the electoral process in Europe, as it becomes a legitimate party, political choice for center-right and conservative electorate across many countries, the fringe elements of these parties will feel that they are no longer really capable of expressing themselves in an open forum in these parties. This is really not a novel phenomenon. In the '60s and the '70s in Europe the rise of left-wing extremism was in many ways prompted by the failure of the more extremist left-wing political organizations that really effect any change in the process".*

The (new) messianic and evangelical approach of the Christian fundamentalism can find a voice inside the legitimate political arena with an alliance with such political parties and inside the mentioned social groups a lot of followers due the fact that these movements are deeply involved in the society offering real solutions ,(from help for the seniors to support for students).

6) Who are them?

It is time to use the right words:

I)   White Christian Fundamentalists and that describes a dangerous social group that overlaps with the neo-nazi but it is bigger than them

II) Civil war and not terrorism. If an Iraqi kills for political reasons other Iraqi in Iraq or if a Lebanese kills other Lebanese in Lebanon and so on we do not use the term terrorism but civil war. Why we cannot use it if a US citizen kills US citizens in the USA or a European kills Europeans in the EU?

Once we assumed that, (WCF involved in a civil war), we can try to understand who them are.

We suggested some dates:

4/19 Oklahoma City
1/8 Tucson
7/22 Utoya and Oslo

And we consider this as part of a bigger conflict that we are used to describe with 9/11 but we should start to consider to have a dimension also in 9/15 when the New York-based Lehman Brothers Holdings Inc. bankrupted and millions that had a life ruined or that were forced to dramatically reduce their living style and hopes for the future.
These groups are filling a political and social vacuum and for that reason we can consider them as NSA, s, (VI).
They are extremely dangerous because able to reach the "hearth and the mind" of the L Generation, REMD and WMD.
Working in the legitimate political arena with conservative and populist parties can influence governments based on fragile coalitions and under pressure due the economic situations.
Their populist agenda based on the code word "security", (against criminality, against the lost of the life style, against the reduced welfare), have a magic appeal.

7) How to react?

The EU and the USA have all they need to react and to win and we do not need to repeat the same error to stigmatize someone as the "final enemy".

Surely we need to re-focus part of the efforts of our intelligence and security forces on the fight against groups that want to make violent attacks.

But both our political and economic systems embodied the anti-virus and they embodied it now.

It is only to find the political wish and courage to do it.

For example:

    a) Retirement
    b) An interesting collection of data that show a different future can be found in "The global aging preparedness index",(VI). It seems that the future of our welfare is not as dramatic as we think even if we will face some reductions. But also that is not so sure if we consider three elements that are unlucky underestimated : I) our expectations for an active and healthy life are increasing. To be clear: if the movie industries as well as that of tourism and fashion are targeting the senior group of the society to show them that a "new" life of fun and sex is possible we can also legitimately expect that the same person has also the energy to work a bit longer
    II) The technology will reduce the physical effort we need to work This simply means an easier longer productive life
    III) The immigration will increase the number of workers

b) Welfare

It is time that our elected elites find the courage to face lobbies and to renounce to an incredible amount of money camouflaged as consulting, jobs and electoral subventions. It is strange and a short term vision to talk only and only about a reduction of the supplied welfare. As it will be only short term populism to talk only about the profits of the capitalism. As usual the thru is in the middle.

It is time to a real saving achieved with a sustainable reduction of the profits of the pharmaceutical industry.

We agree that the pharmaceutical industry must repay its R&D and needs also a ROI able to pay the future research. But there is a limit.

We can easily save billion of euro without affecting the capacity of future R&D.

How?
There is a lot of products where the industry has yet achieved ,(and since years),its ROI and only a de fact cartel united with the gain of part of the elected elites block any effort of rationalization that means a sharp reduction of the costs with the same supply to citizens.

The EU on 2011 passed a law that obliges the producers of computers, mobile phone, and camcorder to produce only one model of device to charge batteries. This will mean a lot of money saved by the clients without affecting the ROI of the producers.

We can do the same for a lot of products supplied to the pharmaceutical industry. Some examples

- Why do we have not a unique sensor for the device to measure sugar in the blood instead of the illogic situations where if a producer produces 4 devices we have 4 different sensors?

- Why we cannot have a unique syringe for insulin instead of the around 25 existing models?

- One standard of the needles

We are talking about diabetes because one of the disease with the bigger impact in the population. If we achieve a standard that does not cost any additional investments and does not affect the ROI of the producers we simply save billions of Euros without reducing the supply to diabetics.

If we multiply it to a lot of equivalent products for other diseases we can find a lot of the money that we need for.

But to do that means to reduce the profit of the pharmaceutical industry and the money for some of the elected elites´, our politicians. It seems a populist approach but it is not. It is the only approach to avoid to pay a higher price in term of our freedom because each reduction in the supply of welfare, (to save the benefits of industries and some politicians), will give power to the message issued by the far right.

c) The conservatives

The moderate conservative parties must stop the right extremism and avoid any overlapping with these social forces that are supporting them. If in the short term that means to lose votes in the long term this will be a gain for them as well as for the democracy.

d) Labor market, (I)

One of the last consequences of 9/15 is that China and other export oriented economies were forced to increase the internal demand. One of the consequences was and is to increase the wages. If the works gain more the same persons have more money to spend as clients. That is, not more not less. In the EU we can have a law for a European minimum wage and this will generate the following benefits:

I. To reduce hate toward the new EU Countries due the industrial re-location and the loss of jobs.

II. To save the purchasing power of the "old" EU Countries

III. To increase that of the new EU Countries and the related market

IV. To cut a powerful element of propaganda for the Christian fundamentalists

e) Labor Market, (II)

There is a lot of hypocrisy when we talk about child labors and pollution. Instead to waste money in conferences that produce a lot in term of media coverage but a few in terms of solutions we can add some "import taxes". For example :
I) Pollution Import Tax : if a country is not working to achieve the Copenhagen standards its export will face an import pollution tax like the carbon tax

II) Child Labor Tax : if a country is using child labor its export will be taxed to finance NGO´s and aid programs to support children

III) Gender discrimination tax : if in a country there a gender based discrimination its import will be taxed to pay programs ,(for example micro-credits), to support local women.

These import taxes will reduce the competitive advantage of a cheaper production and make exports less competitive. The political advantages will be both for the EU workers and for the workers in these countries.

f) Financial Speculations

There is a lot of hypocrisy in Germany where a law prevents the investments in a lot of high-risk and speculative derivates but, (de facto), allows the German banks to offer these products thanks to their branches in London or New York or Milan.
It is not the 1st time that we assist to this kind of "speculation" and to read Braudel about what in London or Amsterdam in the XVI or XVII can confirm it.

It is to create some limits, for example

:

a) to reduce the maximum leverage and to increase the real amount of money to invest. For example not like today 1:20 where with 1 euro you can invest for 20 but, for example, 3:10 and that means to have 3 euro for a leverage of 10.
b) To oblige to buy the physical asset of commodities and not only a contract and to force a minimum period before the reselling. If someone will sell before that period this will be considered a speculative investment and the taxation will be 2 or 3 times higher. This will be a deterrent.

The social benefits of this sustainable financial engineering are clear and this will not affect the stock markets as well as not the capitalism and the future of our economies.

These are only examples that show us how it can be easy to react. It is only a matter of political wish.

8) Conclusion

The Christian fundamentalism can grow in the last ten years thanks to a spread sense of fear and lack of hope in the future that generated a general social apathy. If we not react we will face a civil war inside our societies where some of us will fight for the values of a democratic ,pluralistic society with a sustainable economy and other for a new version of a religious ,(Christian fundamentalist), dominated society where the diversity is a reason to be excluded ,(if not to be killed).

We have now all the energies and the resources we need to fight back but we have to avoid the error we made after 9/11. We do not face an internal "clash of civilization", where the term "civilization" means a different vision of a society. We face a social disease and even if we need to re-focus some of our intelligence and security services on it the winning answer can be only social and economic.

It is upon to us to awake!

Notes:

(I) About the NSA´s : http://prosumerzen.net/category/from-geopolitics-to-biopsherepolitics/no-state-actors-nsa/
(II) http://prosumerzen.net/2011/06/24/post-%e2%80%93osama-better-post-al-qa%e2%80%99ida/
(III) http://prosumerzen.net/2011/05/27/mit-der-nase-volle-indignados-indignati-%e2%80%a6with-broken-balls/
(IV) Homi Karas , " The emerging middle class in developing countries" , OECD Development Centre Working paper N. 285 January 2010
(V) Stratfor 25-7-2011
(VI) R. Jackson , N. Howe ,K. Nakashima :" The global aging preparedness index" –Center for Strategic and International Studies ,October 2010.

(Form of NSA: States within States)

Chap. 47 -The Islands, (The Nine Nations of North America)

June 28, 2011

The Nine Nations of North America, (by a Max J / 2009)

Hemingway... Miami Vice... Miami CSI ... and more.

Welcome into THE ISLANDS, one of the nine North American Nations,(I).

The territory : Florida , Bahamas, Greater Antilles, Puerto Rico, Cuba, Haiti, Netherland Antilles, Lesser Antilles, Jamaica and the northern coast of Venezuela , (including Caracas).

It is better to start thinking to a bridge. In 1934 Henry Flagler began to implement a bridge from Key West to Havana. This bridge could sharply modify the history of the region but in

1935 a hurricane wiped out 45 miles of railroad track and trestle and forced to abandon the project.Islands are a bridge and these are a special one because one between the North and the South America that when united generate the so-called Western Hemisphere.
Once a mayor of Miami, (Maurice Ferré) ,told that the town was the capital of Latin America. At least is one of the capitals ....

And we go ahead with our story thinking to Miami Vice, (the ′80′s of the XX). The serial made a revolution because it was the first where each episode was structured and directed like a film.

From the locations to the soundtracks,(Phil Collins, U2, Sade),all was so stylish and it was Italian style from Ferrari to Armani.

Let′s imagine a remake in the ′20′s of the XXI. Maybe not anymore a Ferrari but a German car like Lamborghini, (eh, yes...this is globalization. Lamborghini is produced near Modena in Italy but the owner is in Audi in Ingolstadt, Germany).

Maybe not anymore Armani but Ralph Lauren ...not a Rolex but a Panerai and so on.

New icons for the same need and we call it fashion that is the only real traversal language. But, at the end, this is not so important.

If we focus on the two caps, (Rico and Tabs), surely now they had to face new enemies and have new friends.

In the '80's of the XX it was "Post Cold War time with the USSR",(the first to use the term "post cold war" was Nixon in 1972), and the enemies were weapons and drug dealers. And sometime the CIA forced to free them because they were useful for the national security in the bloody wars in Central America, (we all remember Contras, Noriega, Castro, De Buisson, Cardinal Romero...).

But today?

If we talk about drugs maybe we have to focus on the Mexican cartels and if we think to weapons to the "Big Gangs" that from Buenos Aires to Montreal are the network of street gangs.

But not only them. Drug and weapons are "old", (even if still extremely), businesses and in the '20's of the XXI is better if we focus on the new ones.

We can describe them as NSA, or parallel power of sub-national powers, (II).

When we talk of the most sophisticated among them we find that The Islands are one of the corners of the hearth with the highest concentration.

Who are them?

- SFW,(Sovereign Wealth Funds), in the Carribe ,(offshore)
- PSF,(Private Security Forces), in Panama
- NSA,(Not State Actors), in the Cayman

New players for new dimensions need new gateway to communicate and that means also new gateway to the South America and to the world.

But we need to add other actors to the scenario.

Let´s focus on the "Saudi Arabia" of the bio-fuel: Cuba and its sugar cane.

In Havana the Castro Brothers, (please always to keep in mind that Fidel Castro is the only man in the list of the Forbes Billionaires in this part of the region. Not surprising for a revolutionary that always loved Rolex. Yes...if the devil dresses Prada...Castro dresses Rolex), are among whom who the most will benefit from 9/11.

How?
One of the most lasting consequences of 9/11 will be the shift to bio-fuel. The imperatives in term of security have made more than the warnings about the climate change.

Cuba is plenty of sugar… But not only this.

Another consequence of 9/11 was a long economic crisis that forced too many countries to save in term of the costs for the health care.

Havana has one of the most advanced industries of the world when we talk about vaccines and its doctors and para-medics are among the best in the world. In other terms Cuba can supply both more affordable drugs and cheaper high quality clinics for the patients from the entire world.

This will be a sustainable way to reduce costs without reducing the quality of the care.

To be clear Cuba can be a future global player when we talk about energy, (bio-fuel), and about health care, (drugs and clinics).Something extremely important for a country that is living a miserable present. By the way to see how the situation is bad we must focus on the fact that any photo and text used to promote the tourism never mention the present but talk about a "legendary" past.

We are talking about new players and new links with the world and what we have told about Cuba introduces to us an example of these new players, protagonists.

Who? Doctors and para-medics are among the wealthiest, (after the oligarchy of the leading party), and this because the work abroad under Governative projects that are part of the foreign policy, (for example in Venezuela).

These people gain more than the normal Cuban and they are also mentally trained to be in touch with the world because, as doctors, need to update themselves. But not only Cuba.

Ina world where the NSA´s have reached their final evolution in a process that started centuries ago, (III), the network of offshore jurisdictions is a strategic place. And these Islands are so near to the banking hubs of Panama and Miami and to the know-how of the lawyers in Miami that the NSA´s cannot afford to avoid to locate there, (or at least to have in the region part of their structures).

And last but not least we have not to forget special luxury cruise ships that since around ten years are de facto small towns where around 10.000 privileged people are living and connecting with the world.

Soon the evolution of these ships will be something like an ideal place to live or run a business, a friendly, safe and secure community with large areas of open space and extensive entertainment and recreational facilities. Imagine this community continually moving around the world. **A state-of-the-art vessel with a design length of 4,500 feet, a width of 750 feet, and a height of 350 feet. The design concepts include a mobile modern city featuring luxurious living, an extensive duty-free international shopping mall, and a full 1.7 million square foot floor** set aside for various companies to showcase their products.

This vessel would not be a cruise ship, it is proposed to be a unique place to live, work, retire, vacation, or visit. The proposed voyage would continuously circle the globe, covering most of the world's coastal regions. Its large fleet of commuter aircraft and hydrofoils would ferry residents and visitors to and from shore. The airport on the ship's top deck would serve private and small commercial aircraft (up to about 40 passengers each). The proposed vessel's superstructure, rising twenty-five stories above its broad main deck, would house residential space, a library, schools, and a first-class hospital in addition to retail and wholesale shops, banks, hotels, restaurants, entertainment facilities, casinos, offices, warehouses, and light manufacturing and assembly enterprises. In other words this concept would include a wide array of recreational facilities. A real world-class resort making it a veritable "town of the sea".

A concept ?

Not at all because there are capitals that are working on it. It is only a matter of time. From a technological point of view it can be built today but the real and only problem is political and that belongs to the NSA´s world.

The Islands…one of the hottest spot in the world where our beloved Rico and Tabs , in the version for the ´20´s of the XXI, have to face la crème de la crème of the anti-democratic and criminal NSA´s to protect the citizens as well as the NSA´s involved in a positive empowerment of the international order.

A lot more then sunny beaches for retirement, at least in the "post cold war world without the USSR", are it?

Notes:

(I) The 1st article at at : http://prosumerzen.net/2011/06/16/obama-15-06-2011-and-the-9-nations-of-the-usa-111/
(II)
to   download   a   list   of   the   existing   21   kinds   of   NSA´s   :
http://prosumerzen.net/2011/05/05/nsa-is-it-correct-the-description-of-the-21-kinds-of-nsa%c2%b4s-2/

(III)
about the historical evolution of the NSA´s

http://prosumerzen.net/2011/04/22/useuropean-powers-vs-pirates-in-africa/

http://prosumerzen.net/2011/04/20/multinationals-as-no-state-actors-multinazionali-come-no-state-actors-derss/

If you want to know more about the NSA at : http://prosumerzen.net/category/from-geopolitics-to-biopsherepolitics/no-state-actors-nsa/

(Form of NSA: Functional Organizations)

Chap. 48 - ICC WANTED: Gadhafi

May 20, 2011

The International Criminal Court, (ICC), has issued international warrants for the three top officials of the regime: Muammar al-Qaddafi; his son Seif al-Islam; and his brother-in-law, the head of Libyan military intelligence, Abdullah al-Sanousi.
They are accused of crimes against humanity during the revolt.

This is great but it is unlucky another of the "bottle neck" that the world face because we have not global institutions with not only a mandate but also the instruments to apply it.

There are some critics that blame the ICC for this action because it can force Gadhafi to fight till the end, (and this increasing the number of causalities), instead to search a solution with an exile. This kind of critics has not room simply because only 114 countries have signed the convention of the ICC and Gadhafi & Co. can chose among a lot of countries, starting with his supporter President Chavez, (see solution 3).

From a practical point of view the problem is: **who will arrest the three and carry them to The Hague for the process?**

The ICC has not a police unit to execute it. Additionally inside the UN Resolution 1973, (I), there is not any mention of the fact that all governments must enforce the ICC arrest warrants related to Libya.

Realistically we face three solutions, pardon four.

Solution 1: they surrender to the National Transition Council or are captured by the NTC. Then the NTC deliver them to the ICC. Not a lot probable.

Solution 2: an internal golpe and someone of the regime forces that want to use the warrants as a political alibi to change the regime and send them to the ICC.This with the goal to negotiate some solution with the NTC and to save the actors of the golpe. It can be possible.

Solution 3: the 114 countries that have signed the Convention are forced to arrest someone with a warrant if the person is in the territory of the country. Unlucky Gadhafi & Co have the option to choose among the other 67 countries in the world. In this case the hosting country can chose if to arrest or not. If they do it will be as a courtesy and if they do not do they do not face sanctions. The USA is among the not signatory countries as well as Venezuela and dozens in Africa. If we exclude the USA they are all countries where Gadhafi & Co. can find a more than comfortable hospitality, (we consider Caracas as a hot spot for his choice to exile). Again: not a lot probable that they will be carried by the hosting country to the ICC court.

Solution 4: to capture Gadhafi the ICC needs someone that can execute the mandate. This explains why the NATO is so thrilled about this decision.

First of all it gives a new political support of its work because of the reason of the warrant.

Secondarily, and not less important, **it supplies a legal and political reason to send troops on the field with the excuse to capture the leadership of the regime.** It will be not the first "extensive interpretation" of the Resolution 1973 by the NATO because the first was to extend the mandate from a "No-fly zone" to a "No fly/drive

zone".
Now the NATO could have the justification to send troops. It
could   have.
But maybe the first to be not so happy of this evolution are
the USA.

The Republican will not accept either an interference of the
ICC in a NATO military operation not to execute an ICC
warrant because Washington did not and for the near future
does not sign the Convention and does not accept the ICC
authority.
The same for Berlin that will be more than cold about the
option to send troops, (not mention the fact that if Germany
will agree on it de fact will contradict its vote at the UN
Security Council).

This action can generate a lot of problems.

It is sure that the ICC needs diplomatic as well as
operational support to execute the warrant.

From a diplomatic point of view the first place to ask for it is
the Security Council where the vote will be not sure.

- China and Russia will see it as interference inside the
sovereignty.

- Russia stated that Moscow never supports any resolution
against Assad and consequently the Russian will be
concerned that if they authorize the NATO to arrest Gadhafi
this could be a precedent for the Syrian President.

- The USA both for the internal opposition of the Republican
to any acts that endorse the ICC and for the fear to create a
precedent for Israel, (read the UN forces in Lebanon).

- Among other members,(not permanent),inside the Security Council a lot of them either will vote against or with their abstention will make harder to find a decision, for example :

- Germany: Berlin abstained to vote and if now Germany supports the decision that the UN Resolution 1973 must add a mandate to the NATO, (like in Yugoslavia in 1990), to arrest the leadership of the regime this will require an operational engagement of its army and it will contradict its initial position, (giving to Paris and London a political leadership inside the EU that the yet frustrated German leadership does not want to give)

- The Nations of the Arab League: rumors inside the intelligence community tell that they supported the ICC to find evidences but it will be hard to think that they will support the warrant. This because doing it they will create a dangerous precedent for a warrant against Sudan's President Omar al-Bashir, who, despite being the subject of an arrest warrant for atrocities in Darfur, has been supported by the Arab League that does not execute the warrant.

- Countries like Venezuela will refuse it because President Chavez would offer Qaddafi the opportunity to expose the long-term cooperation he enjoyed in Africa as well as in the Arab world.

An interesting and dangerous **legal and operational „neck of bottle" t**hat will be remembered long time after the end of the war and that will supply one of the most important consequences of the conflict at least inside the international relations, (the second is that about the Libyan SWF ,(II)).

Notes:

(I) The integral text of the Un Resolution 1973
http://prosumerzen.net/category/tarsga-%c2%a9-the-sustainable-risk-management/humpolitics-%c2%a9-sustainable-geopolitics-arga-%c2%a9-anti-risk-global-approach-the-sustainable-risk-management/page/2011/03/19/un-resolution-1973-integral-text/
(II) http://prosumerzen.net/2011/05/18/tactical-warning-libya-opec-swf/

(Form of NSA: Functional Organizations)

Chap.49- V4 ...an INDIPENDENT army for Europe, at least for a part of it...

May 17, 2011

V4?

V4 means the **Visegrad Group**. A group of four EU Countries: Poland, Slovakia, Hungary, Czech Rep. and it is a 20 years old institution named after two 14th century meetings held in Visegrad Castle in present-day Hungary of leaders of the medieval kingdoms of Poland, Hungary and Bohemia.

On 12-5-2011 these four EU and NATO members "simply" created a battle group under the command of Poland and NOT integrated in the NATO as well as not in the (future or " ?futuristic ? "),EU Response Force . By 2016 it will be an **independent military force in the hearth of Europe** even if in 2013 the four countries will start joint military exercises together under the auspices of the NATO Response Force.

Since 1989 these countries felt their strategic future deeply anchored with the EU and the NATO and their analysis was based on the following three main geo-political reasons:

a) They felt that the Russian threat had declined if not dissipated following the fall of the Soviet Union.
b) They felt that their economic future was with the European Union.
c) They believed that membership in NATO, with strong U.S. involvement, would protect their strategic interests.

The event of 12th May is historic for the EU, (and as well for the trans-Atlantic relations), because it shows that the V4 has clearly been shifting away from this analysis,

Why?

A) Russia: Moscow has increased its relative power, (since 1989). And the campaign against Georgia, (2008), plus its extended influence both in other former Soviet States and in Berlin. The V4 underlying fear of Russia has become more intense. On other terms due to their historical memories they are countries that have the least confidence that the Cold War is simply a relic of the past or, if you prefer, an old memory.

B) The EU: the infatuation with Europe, while not gone, has frayed. From economy to international politics. About the economy what is going on since 2008, (including the Greece debt), has raised two vital questions:

- Whether Europe as an entity is viable?

- And whether the reforms proposed to stabilize Europe represent a solution for them or primarily for the Germans, (and to pay the bill to their industries)?

To be clear it is not, by any means, that they have given up the desire to be Europeans inside the EU.

But and at the same time it is logic to understand that these countries would not be uneasy about the direction that Europe was taking. Look, for example at the unease with which Warsaw and Prague are deflecting questions about the eventual date of their entry into the Eurozone. Both are the strongest economies in Central Europe, and neither is (so) enthusiastic about the euro.

About the politics the reason of the UN to refuse a permanent siege to the EU explains all better than one million words.

C) The NATO: too many are wondering if NATO provides a genuine umbrella of security to its members. The NATO strategic concept as was drawn up in November 2010 generated substantial concern and this for two reasons:

I) there was the question of the degree of American commitment to the region, considering that the document sought to expand the alliance's role in non-European theaters of operation. (To be clear the US commitment to protect the North European Plain from a Russian invasion is considered by Poland far below the necessary and, out of hypocrisy, all are starting to feel how uncomfortable is a world without the US Army and to fear it).

II) The general weakness of European militaries meant that, willingness aside, the ability of the Europeans to participate in defending the region is negligible. (but we do not over estimate what is going on with the NATO – with a less American engagement in Libya even if we do not underestimate a dangerous situation where the NATO-without the USA is showing inability to create a coherent strategy and deploy adequate resources).

Additionally there a fourth element:

D) Germany: Germany's commitment to both NATO and the EU has been fraying. The "NATO-without US leadership-but-EU leadership" war in Libya will be remembered less for the fate of Gadhafi than for the fact that this was the first significant strategic break between Germany and France in decades. On other terms since the end of the IIWW the German national strategy has been to remain closely aligned with France. This to create European solidarity and to avoid

Franco-German tensions that had roiled Europe since 1871. This had been a centerpiece of German foreign policy, and it was suspended, at least temporarily. And this to follow an outdated 1860 dream about a special relation between Berlin and Moscow where Berlin can control Siberia.

But this dream, (we can describe it as the growing relations between Germany and Moscow), has raised the warning bells for countries, (like these of the V4), that have only an historic memory of problems from this relation. They see a pro-Moscow Byelorussia, Moldova and Ukraine where Moscow is playing hard using its "organic NSA´s",(I), (the organized crime and the national industrial champions) ,to set the rules either for the internal as well as for the international politics of these countries.

Inside this contest the 12th May decision has generated one of the two realistic examples of a European not-NATO force that can be described as an effective battle group, (the second, despite its problems and weakness, is the Nordic Battle Group /NBG, (II),).

By the way it is not by coincidence that the only of the 18 EU Battle Groups, (EUBG), that is full operative is the NBG and this simply because the Nordic countries share the same concerns as the V4 countries about the future course of Russian power linked to the German visions, the cohesiveness of Europe facing the Germany geo-politics and the commitment of the United States under the new strategic needs of a superpower that is running to a post-oil dimension..

The message is clear: the decision to do this is significant in and of itself!

This because it tells how the V4 considers:

- The Russian power
- The German visions
- The US engagement
- The coherence, (and sustainability). Of the EU

And most important: how they think they can best protect their own security inside the NATO and the EU!

No one wanted it but they are forced to do it…time for the European rhetoric is over and forever and we hope that it will be not over also that for the trans-Atlantic relations. **Now it is time to act but where is the wish? And who has the vision and the credibility to lead the trend?**

It is not by coincidence that the land trapped between Berlin and Moscow, (Poland), has taken the lead of the decision and it is leading the battle group. In July, the Poles will be assuming the EU presidency in one of the union's six-month rotations. The Poles have made clear that one of their main priorities will be Europe's military power. Obviously, little can happen in Europe in six months, but this clearly indicates where Poland's focus is and if nothing happens Warsaw hat is own "personal insurance" thanks to the militarization of the V4 region.

Are we over reading the trends in the region?

We do not think so and even this battle group is a small answer to the threat and no one is thinking able to stop the broken Russian military power this is the only answer to a current post –cold war trend that these nations feel can have a sense.

Which trend? A trend that emerged in 2008 and for that reason we could tell that the cold war ended in that corner of the world only on 2008. The crisis showed how the periphery, (Moscow and Berlin), have a different vision: either their vision of Europe or nothing and the countries at the periphery, (like the V4 or the Nordic ones), has been started to feel unsure.

And, unlucky, geopolitical realities drive consciousness and insecurity and distrust defines this region.

Are we back to the "Intermarium", (III)?

Let´s evaluate the players: Ukraine, Romania, Bulgaria, and Turkey.

At the May 12 defense ministers' meeting, there was discussion of inviting Ukraine to join in. Now it is not the right moment. It was possible till 2000 but now Moscow is blocking it.

And if it is not possible with Ukraine the only option is to go south to the other "natural" members of this geo-political idea.

It means Romania and Bulgaria but the low-level tension between the two countries over the status of Hungarians in Romania makes that difficult, but there is still a lot of room to maneuver.

Logically the question that geopolitically matters the more is whether Ankara will participate or not. A question the Turkish strategists have not in their mind and we have to wait for some evolutions to see this idea to be considered as an option of the Ankara´s strategy.

At the end only Romania and Bulgaria seem to be the only tow that can become partner of the V4 without problems. If this will happens it will be a turning point in the trends of the region.

We do not think that, at least not before 5 years but a lot in Berlin, Washington and Moscow can accelerate this trend.

In any case it represents a new level of concern over an evolving reality where the power of Russia, the weakness of Europe, a NATO that is testing to be a bit less US controlled more than fragmentized, the visions of Germany and the how the USA will back are the ingredients of the geopolitical cocktail in the region.

The end of the NATO and of the EU is the last things the V4 wants to see, but they have now done the last thing they wanted to do. That has an incredible, symbolic political value because we are talking about an **INDIPENDENT** insurance for their life that tells to the world that they less trust Brussels, (if not a future of peace in Europe).

This is something we cannot avoid to think about.

Notes :
(I) About the 21 kinds of NSA´s:
http://prosumerzen.net/2011/05/05/nsa-is-it-correct-the-description-of-the-21-kinds-of-nsa%c2%b4s-2/
(II) the Nordic Battle group, (NBG), is one of eighteen European Union battle groups. It consists of around 2,200 soldiers including officers, with manpower contributed from the five participating countries (Sweden, Finland, Norway, Ireland and Estonia). The military strategic command of the force is done in cooperation with the any suitable of the five Operation Headquarters framework nations at the time for deployment.[1] Denmark has opted out of the Common

Foreign and Security Policy pillar of the EU, hence all battle groups. Norway has negotiated an opt-in to participate, even though it is not an EU member state. The unit uses a modular organization with a mechanized infantry battalion at its core (During NBG 2008 it was the 41. Rapid Reaction Battalion, During NBG 2011 it is the 192. Rapid Reaction Battalion), which has been organized around Norrbottens regemente (I19). During 2011 a framework exists for the integration of additional resources. These resources range from artillery, air defense, and intelligence to additional logistical support. Additional support in the form of air, naval and Special Forces assets will be allocated based on the operational tasks the unit is expected to perform. It consists of around 2.200 units supplied as follow :
• Sweden: 1600
• Finland: 250
• Ireland: 150
• Estonia: 100
• Norway: 100
The NBG is a light armored battle group as its armament shows :
Vehicles
• Mowag Piranha (Armored Personnel carrier)
• BV 309 (Personnel carrier 309)
• RG 32 Galten (High Mobility Wheeled Vehicle)
• XA-203 SISU (Armored Personnel carrier)
• Mercedes-Benz G-Class (Softskin jeep)
Helicopters
• AgustaWestland AW109 (HKP 15)
• Mil Mi-17
Aircraft
• JAS 39 Gripen – (Fighter aircraft)
• C-130 Hercules – (Military transport aircraft)
About its structural weakness : on October 29, 2010 the findings of an official audit by the Swedish National Audit Office was published which concluded with fundamental weaknesses in the organization's logistics capabilities, internal cooperation and personnel supply. According to the National Auditor, Jan Landahl, the Nordic Battle Group also

suffered from inadequate control over expenditures and reporting from the Swedish cabinet to the parliament was also unsatisfactory. The audit office's report found that twice as many Swedish soldiers were assigned to the Battle Group compared to what the 2004 mandate had assigned, and the costs to the Swedish government was in the multiples of what the parliament had been told. In advance of fiscal year 2008 the Swedish Armed Forces were critically underfunded, and this led to Battle Group personnel being dismissed

(III) *"By developing a federal alternative to the European Union to be known popularly as the Intermarium, east central Europe might effectively pool its resources and meet the foreign relations and security challenges unique to the region rather than relying upon far away Brussels in the event of a crisis. Regional federation as exemplified by east central Europe's unique heritage may prove to be just the bridging mechanism needed to accelerate the goal of Pan Europe or provide a safe harbor from conflict in the event of the EU's inability to address future crises.* (Jonathan Levy, 2006) An interesting historical introduction at :<a href=" http://en.wikipedia.org/wiki/Mi%C4%99dzymorze" target="_blank"> http://en.wikipedia.org/wiki/Mi%C4%99dzymorze

In any case **we are not talking** about the so called "Christian Confederation of Intermarium". We refer only to the evolution of the original idea and not to the "utilization" by religious as well as political movements/parties.

(Form of NSA: Functional Organizations)

Chap.50: IMF; what if the chief…?

Each person is innocent till is not proven guilty and we respect this pillar of the justice. For this reason we want to work using a *"what if scenario"*for this article.

Let´s imagine a SA that is:

- One of the three leading nations in the EU
-A nation that is a NATO´s pillar as well as a pillar inside the G7,G8 and G20
-A nation that is permanent member of the UN Security Council
-That has the third nuclear arsenal in the world
- That is member of a special club, (a sort of G3 of the military power), because one of the 3 nations in the world either with deep water capability and international power projection capability
- With an international network of alliances
- World leader for the nuclear energy
- With the 2nd best space technology in the world

And now imagine a person that is

- A leading figure in the second party of this nation
- A leading figure of the progressive parties at worldwide level
- A candidate with real chances to win a presidential election
- The chief of the most powerful Functional Organization, (the IMF), in the world. A States Influenced Non State Actor,

(SINSA).
- Member of elite clubs around the world
-A person that either belongs to the Bureaucratically Elected Elites ,(BTE), an elite elected by the SA´s and to the Politically Elected Elites, (PEE), an elite elected by citizens

And only inside our *"what if scenario"* let´s also imagine that this person is linked to the Trans-national Organized Crime, (TOC), another NSA.

This person has a strong interest for ladies and due to his money and power can find at any Concierge a good adviser to find a prostitute. Additionally because resident in a megalopolis and because of this aptitude it is almost most then sure that he has his "private hot directory" for his bungabunga ´s party.

But this is his private life and we are not bigots and we do not comment it . Till this is something private in his bedroom and the involved subjects are consentient we do not see any problem.

Totally different if there is a rape and totally different if this means a structured link with the organized crime.

On clear text the point is only one : how is fragile this person in the term of a racket ?

It is hard to believe that the TOC did not drill this occasion and once informed about it let all in the hands of some small local gangs specialized on prostitution.

It is more than sure that this escalates till the top level of the TOC and this person become one of their puppet.

It is alarming to see that the intelligence services of two of the biggest and more powerful countries in the world as well as the security service of the IMF did not know this situation.

A lot of seniors officers must supply some embarrassing explications and there is the need , an urgent need ,of some clean up.

Again this is a "*what if scenario*" but if this person will be proven guilty this is also an episode that confirms how the relations between NSA´s are either transversal and above the SA´s.

And in this case how these relations can be dangerous… .

(Form of NSA: Functional Organizations)

Chap.51 - The G8 under a BRICS, (the supposed alternative G5), perspective (1)

(Editorial Note: more than one year later the prestigious Foreign Affairs confirmed this vision in Ruchir Sharma – The Demise of the Rest –FA Vol.91/6 Nov-Dec 2012)

May 30, 2011

Some questions:

A) **Weapons to India, (100 billion US$ market in 10 years)**

The BRICS has 3 world leading countries as weapons producers but India wants to have the USA as supplier from now till 2021.

Why the USA and not Russia, Brasil and China?

And why till 2021 when it seems that around 2015-2020 China will be the biggest economy or the USA will make default?

Maybe it seems only…and no one really believes that…

B) **Energy to China**

China must reduce the supply of energy due to the increase of   prices.
Brasil and Russia are world class energy powerhouses and both BRICS members.

Russia can sell at an astonishing discounted price gas to Ukraine and this because of strategic reasons.

But, it seems, that China has not enough strategic value to reduce the selling price and to help the allied Beijing.

Why?

C) **The UN intervention in Libya**

For some aspects the G8 is more a meeting of the western powers. Russia sharply changed its position, (if we consider the vote about the UN Resolution 1973), and left Germany and its BRICS ally China alone.

It seems that Moscow gives more value to the G8 then to a supposed common policy with China/BRICS.

Why?

D) **Brasil and yuan**

Brasilia supports the Washington´s vision about the yuan.

This contrasts with the "picture" of a united BRICS as the new and alternative global powerhouse, (the alternative G5).

Why?

E) **South Africa and Cote d´Ivoire**

For the 1st time in 10 years Pretoria has nothing to tell about an African crisis, (Cote d´Ivoire), and the lead was run by Paris.

But South Africa as official BRICS member should be at the "zenith" of its power as African global power house.

Why?

The answers will draw a different picture of the so called and more supposed then real alternative G5, the BRICS.

The answers on the 2nd part of this article.

(Form of NSA: Functional Organizations)

Chap.52 -The G8 under a BRICS, (the supposed alternative G5), perspective (2)

(Editorial Note: more than one year later the prestigious Foreign Affairs confirmed this vision in Ruchir Sharma – The Demise of the Rest –FA Vol.91/6 Nov-Dec 2012)

June 1, 2011

In the 1st section of this article we asked some question that can spread a new light about the BRICS real status as alternative, (G5?), powerhouse.

A) Weapons to India, (100 billion US$ market in 10 years)

The BRICS has 3 world leading countries as weapons producers but India wants to have the USA as supplier from now till 2021.

- Why the USA and not Russia, Brasil and China?

The UN refusals to have the EU as a permanent member of the Security Council is an example that explain why cannot be a EU weapon.

About Russia the Russians are not as reliable as seller, at least for the Indians, because of their "last minute „renegotiation of the price to sell to New Delhi an old carrier. Additionally both Russia and China offer fighters that are cheaper but far away from the US technology.

This is also an interesting ("indirect") evidence of the real value of the Russian and Chinese high-tech weapons face the alarmism about a new super China or about the BRICS as a military powerhouse able to challenge the world.

"Simply" the day that India can afford to pay for the best it buys Made in the USA and this despite the BRICS...

- And why till 2021 when it seems that around 2015-2020 China will be the biggest economy or the USA will make default?

Maybe because someone is reading the metrics that count. These metrics tells that China around 2015-2018 will have a GDP pro capita of 17.000 USD, (1975 PPC), and that its population on 2030 will be older of that of the USA. The first data means that China in 2021 will not achieve the indispensable 9% GPD growth to maintain the social order and the second will make it worst.

The USA have all the resources to solve the deficits as were done in the period 1992-1998.

B) Energy to China

China must reduce the supply of energy due to the increase of prices.

Brasil and Russia are world class energy powerhouses and both BRICS members. Russia can sell at an astonishing discounted price gas to Ukraine and this because of strategic reasons. But, it seems, that China has not enough strategic value to reduce the selling price and to help the allied Beijing.

Why?

Brazil is a powerhouse either about oil and gas or about bio-energy. Unlucky its bio-energy at the moment cannot help China because Beijing has not the infrastructure to deliver it and the Chinese not the hardware, (cars, trucks...), to use it. Its oil and gas cannot be sold at a discounted price simply because Made in Brazil is fighting against Made in China. In other words, we are in a "just-in-time" world and any persistent "bottle neck" in the production/delivering forces to change suppliers otherwise the supply chain will crash. If China will have problems to deliver the buyers will accept to pay a bit more but to buy in more reliable countries, for example Brazil.

And this for Brasilia is more important than the cohesion of a Beijing -led- BRICS.

Russia could help China selling at a discounted price like, for example, with Ukraine. But, despite the BRICS rhetoric, has not reasons to do it.

In other words Russia has its own strategic interest if China is not so strong, (starting from the ethnic invasion in Siberia).

C) The UN intervention in Libya

For some aspects the G8 is more a meeting of the western powers. Russia sharply changed its position, (if we consider the vote about the UN Resolution 1973), and left Germany and its BRICS ally China alone. It seems that Moscow gives more value to the G8 then to a supposed common policy with China/BRICS.

Why?

Here is important to understand of what we are talking about when we talk about the G8.

IF the benchmark to be member of the G8 is the importance as world economy we have to change a lot.

The actual G8 , (into the brackets the rank as world economy) : The USA,(1), Japan,(3), Germany,(4), France,(5),the UK (6),Italy,(8),Russia,(9),Canada,(10)

The REAL G8 should be : The USA (1), China (2), Japan,(3), Germany,(4), France,(5),the UK (6),Brasil(7), Italy(8)

That means that Canada and Russia are not part of the "club". It is clear that Moscow is in the G8 more for its political value linked to the fact to be the 2nd nuclear power of the world and to have enormous energetic reserves and this means **that Italy and Canada must leave** the G...or to transform it in a G10 but this will be pathetic.

During the last G8 the Russian President changed the official policy about Libya, (leaving Germany and China alone), and felt comfortable in what someone describe as the "elite club of the West". In any case his words were not these inspired by a common BRICS international politics.

Russia is aware that is international status over estimate its real power and if Moscow has to decide between the G8 and the BRICS ...it decides for the G8.

D) Brasil and yuan

Brasilia supports the Washington´s vision about the yuan. This contrasts with the "picture" of a united BRICS as the new and alternative global powerhouse, (the alternative G5).

Why?

Simply because there is not a political wish to change. The problem is not to change the so called "(American) liberal world order" but to have more power inside it. We described why it is not politically possible to shift to a new and alternative currency, (I), and again this counts for Brasilia more than the "BRICS axes".

E) South Africa and Cote d´Ivoire

For the first time in 10 years Pretoria has nothing to tell about an African crisis, (Cote d´Ivoire), and the lead was run by Paris. But South Africa as official BRICS member should be at the "zenith" of its power as African global powerhouse. Why?

To have Pretoria on board in the BRICS, (and to prefer S. Africa to Turkey, II), answers to the strategic Beijing´s plan about Africa.

Not only as a continent where it is possible to find commodities or a market but also, and more important in a middle term vision, (2015-2020), the last reservoir of low cost job. Or, in other words, Africa will be the next "world inflation killer" thanks to a low cost production as it was China in the last 25 years. The rising production costs ,(read it the rising wages to maintain the social order), are affecting this Chinese role if we consider Laos, Vietnam, Cambodia, Madagascar, South Africa, Bangladesh we have yet countries cheaper than China.

But if Pretoria is losing this leading role, (see Cote d´Ivoire), and soon China will face a more western friendly Libyan power in Africa, (III), this will reduce a lot of Beijing´s strategic power.

This world is not a G0 world but a **GX** world and it is also a world where the main players n the 38 geopolitical exchequers are more interested on preserving the order than on shaping it.

But about the different "**G-relevant**", (from the G8 to the G-organized crime), we will talk in the 3rd section of this article.

Notes:

(I)   http://prosumerzen.net/2011/05/24/the-new-chapter-of-the-war-between-no-state-actors-and-state-actors-the-currency-war-2/

(II)   http://prosumerzen.net/2011/04/14/ankarapretoria-brics/

(III)   http://prosumerzen.net/2011/05/18/tactical-warning-libya-opec-swf/

(Form of NSA: Functional Organizations)

Chap. 53 It is not time for BRICS+V (=Venezuela)

(Editorial Note: more than one year later the prestigious Foreign Affairs confirmed this vision in Ruchir Sharma – The Demise of the Rest –FA Vol.91/6 Nov-Dec 2012)

July 6, 2011

Caracas: Chinese and Russian soldiers participated in the parade for the celebration of the 200th of Venezuela.

There is no need to give to this event any political meaning that over estimate it. And not at all to think to a BRICSV.

Fact 1: Venezuela refines 75% of its oil in the USA because due to its geological structure only in the USA it is possible to find refineries able to refine this oil. If the USA blocks it neither China nor Russia and not Iran can refine it

Fact 2: The USA is the biggest client with 85% of the generated revenue. Caracas cannot afford to lose Washington as well as "to say no" simply because there are no alternative clients, (see Fact 1). (In a sentence : the sell to the USA paid 85% of the cost of the parade and 85% of the energy needed to broadcast the 55 minutes Chavez's speech ... This has paid all and not the march of the Russian and Chinese soldiers)

Fact 3: despite the dramatic, (I), energy crisis in China Chavez did not send one gallon of oil at discounted price.

Fact 4: despite the common "anti-USA & Israel" rhetoric Chavez sells gasoline to Iran at the same price of the others, (on average plus 25% on the international price)

Fact 5: despite the energetic crisis in Russia, (YES in Russia, II), Chavez did not send a gallon at discounted price.

Fact 6: despite the Intra-American rhetoric Brazil did not sell 1 Kg of rice at discounted price to Chavez and this despite the food problems in Venezuela. By the way also China did no sell 1 kg of apple at discounted price.

Rhetoric is one thing but facts are life.

These facts prove that that parade means less than nothing and we will not see the BRICS**V**.

Notes

(I) http://prosumerzen.net/2011/05/18/tactical-warning-china-potential-production-problems-and-reduced-demands/

(II) http://prosumerzen.net/2011/05/03/tactical-warning-gasoline-crisis-in-russia/

(Form of NSA: Global Diaspora)

Paolo Dealberti

Chap.54- Spy…spy…oh my dear spy 1/2

January 25, 2011

This is not a story that involves Aston Martin, attractive Englishman and sophisticated Ladies, Beluga caviar and Dom Perignon.

Not at all. We talk about chips and photovoltaic hardware for cars that have to use renewable energy.

Made in France technology by Renault. This time is different.

Paris prosecutor Jean-Claude Marin on Jan. 14 began an inquiry into allegations of commercial espionage carried out against French carmaker Renault .President Sarkozy,(this was the 1st time),has issued an executive order and the French intelligence is also involved to find evidences.

This affair is something new ,why ?

One reason is that for the 1st time 3 Top Managers are involved and this is unusual. This is not the way used by the Chinese Intelligence that acts using a "**mosaic strategy**". What is that ? China is used to work with a "mosaic strategy" which is a wholly different paradigm than that of the West. Instead of recruiting a few high-level sources, the Chinese recruit as many low-level operatives as possible who are charged with vacuuming up all available open-source information and compiling and analyzing the innumerable elements of intelligence to assemble a complete picture. This method fits well with the Chinese labor and not capital intensive historical way to work, which is characterized by countless thousands of capable and skilled people working overseas as well as thousands more analyzing various pieces of the mosaic back home. As told this time they recruited 3 Top Managers and paid them around 1 million € and this a total different approach.

But this is not the most important element of the story…

According to some "confidential rumors" that Prosumerzen was able to collect inside the intelligence community there is a story behind the story…and that is the most interesting one!

According to those rumors it seems **that second- and third-generation Chinese who have assimilated in a new culture are rarely willing to spy, and the Chinese government has much less leverage over this segment of the ethnic-Chinese population living overseas.**

Who are them?

They are around 100 hundred million people described as " **World China**" and they are the worldwide Chinese Diaspora. An important and strategic asset of the Chinese global power as well described by Kotkin ,(1).

And if those rumors are real we are facing an amazing trend that represents a dramatic change in the equation of global powers with the rising of a new and ,(almost),unknown variable.

This will be evaluated in the 2nd part of this article.

(1) "Tribes: How Race, Religion and Identity Determine Success in the New Global Economy "- (1994) by Joel Kotkin

(Form of NSA: Global Diaspora)

Chap.55-Spy...spy...oh my dear spy 2/2

February 6, 2011

As told in the 1st part of this article ,(1), we have found "confidential rumors" inside the intelligence community and if the dots are connected we can see an interesting scenario. A trend that it is mostly unknown but that can affect the "soft power",(2),of Beijing.

This new dimension is affecting 4 realities :

1) World China
2) The internal Chinese demographic trends
3) The demographic trends in Central Asia and in Siberia
4) The Organized Crime either as organic to the political power and as Not State Actor , (NSA)

1) World China

The worldwide Chinese Diaspora, (known as World China),is a strategic asset for the Beijing global power projection and here we talk about the reduced "soft power" ,(less appeal), to those Communities. This is a problem because the mentioned Communities can be the "Trojan horse" used to invest in a Country avoiding the negative feedback originated by the variable of the "national security". We all know that the Chinese national oil Company cannot buy an American oil company due to concerns raised by the national security. The question is : and when a rich local Sino-American, (member of the World China), and not a State controlled Company would like to buy an oil company in the USA (or anywhere) ?

Another way where an influent soft power can transform the Diaspora in a precious asset is when the members press their elected to be more benign and/or positive toward Beijing, (and also when they manifest pro-China). Not mention the advantages in term either of money remittances /investments at home and of investments in the Chinese stock markets by members of the Diaspora and this using Financial institutions located aboard, (only to say : if they start to show an interest on yuan how many banks will find an interesting marketing option to offer also financial products issued in the Chinese currency …).

2) The internal Chinese demographic trends

The Chinese ratio Man/Woman is 107,9 and this means that for 100 Women we have 107.9 Men. It is forecasted that in the next 10 years this will mean that around 140 million of men will not find a wife. The consequent social instability is more than clear. Due problems like the language it will be ,on average, harder to find Women outside the Diaspora. In this contest if the Motherland has less appeal it will mean less Women that want to back to China.

3) The demographic trends in Central Asia and Siberia

A key to understand is Lattimore,(3),and to traslate it in the XXI starting to what is going on since 1997 in the Free Trade Zone between Blagoveshchensk and Heihe. The most important strategic "time bomb" for Moscow is the risk to lose Siberia due to the fact that after 2040 it will not possible to have a Russian majority in the territories after the Urals. Among them Siberia. We are aware that in the XXI Siberia has less strategic value than in the mid XIX,(4), or in the early XX,(5), but at the same tine Moscow cannot think to lose this control. The psychological shock and the reduction of the geo-strategic power due to the fact to back to a territory as it was before XV will be inacceptable. In a situation where the Beijing appeal in term of soft power to the Diaspora in those region could be reduced we assist to a reshape of the cards. To better understand it we have to keep in mind that in the 1996,(6),Beijing issued an alarm about a 3rd region ,(Inner Mongolia), shaped by separatist movements and that it is clear that what told about the Taiwanese separatism has a stringent value for any region of the country. If we will face a reduced appeal it will made a less problematic situation for Moscow and ,maybe, it could be even possible to think to some special jurisdiction like that we have now in the Hebraic Enclave of Birobidzan,(outhern Siberia) . The consequence will be a reduced influence for Beijing and an example for the inner separatism.

4) The Organized Crime either as organic to the political power and as Not State Authority , (NSA)

An interesting element is to remember the former Chinese President Jiang Zemin,(1993-2003). His fundamental military reforms were stripping the military of much of its business empire. At the time, the state — while funding the military — assumed that military-run industry would supplement the defense budget. In short, the military ran industries, and the profits were used to support local and regional defense needs. That encouraged the military elite´to contribute to China's economic growth. It also led to corruption and a military where regional and local military commanders were at risk of becoming more intent on their business, (and political parallel), empires than on the country's national defense and the China's central leadership saw troubling parallels to older Chinese history, **when regional warlords emerged**. It was 2003…regional warlords in China. The current leadership has modified the situation but it is also realistic to assume **that some of the mentioned PARALLEL power did not vanished.**

If we keep in mind this variable we can better evaluate what we told in "Smuggling in China",(7), when we supposed a parallel with the OC in Russia as described by some "rumors" inside the intelligence community about the Kremlin internal wars and the "search" for something like "the Minister of Organized Crime".

If a parallel could be draw and if inside this parallel we can think to some kind of Not State Actors again we can understand how can be a problem to have less soft power inside the Diaspora.

We want to avoid any misunderstanding. The Chinese Diaspora it is NOT AT ALL an "ensemble" of state / security services linked economic tycoons, spies, war lords and criminals...not at all !

We talk of hundred million of honest and laborious people perfectly integrated and loyals to their new lands.

We are talking of a possible reduced soft power that can affect the global Chinese power.

A new and almost unknown variable in the geo-political world.

Notes:

1- "Spy..spy..oh my dear spy 1/2 " – January 25, 2011 in Prosumerzen / Humpolitics
2- We consider the „soft power" as described by the Harvard Professor Joseph Nye Jr.
3- Lattimore , The Frontier – 1947
4-Ratzel , Politische Geographie -1879
5-McKinder- Heathland
6-„ a 3rd Chinese Region rings Separatist Alarm" , 6-7-1996 Reuters /IHT
7-Smuggling in China – Prosumerzen /Geo-politics 30-12-2010

(From of NSA: Transnational Organized Crime)

Chap. 56 - Tunisia the illegal flow of ....

February 14, 2011

The current institutional vacuum is helping the Transnational Organized Crime, (TOC), that has been started again the illegal flow of people.

In a less political correct way we can describe it as the trading of humans or…the new slavery

This situation has also a deep political meaning. Despite a revolution and a change of regime the OC in Tunisia can do its own business and can do it easier due to the vacuum. On political terms this means that, unlucky, the structure of the REAL power behind and around this traffic is always on the field and it has not suffered.

This real and parallel power will have its influence on the new political order. We must keep in mind it and track who is making it to check with whom is linked. We must be aware of it and track this trend to support who can be against it and help to reduce the power of the OC.

It is clear that this problem has ONLY a political solution. To send money and/or to send Police Officers, (as requested to Italy),is useful but it is only a temporary solution suited for the emergency.

But medium and long term solutions can be only political ones and if "on board" we will have who gains from this traffic and with an alliance q with the OC, well no solutions will be found.

Now is time for a second revolution: that against the TOC.

The same TOC that affects also our life in our towns, (not forget it !).

(From of NSA: Global Diaspora)

Chap.57- World China: Italy & Spain

February 14, 2011

We have yet mentioned about the World China (I, II)

2 interesting data :

a) Spain: more than 63.000 Companies are owned by Chinese immigrants (World China). And this create that biggest industrial zone in the EU, (near Madrid with more than 2.000 companies)

b) Italy: in Veneto ,(a region stronghold of the federalist party "Lega Nord"), the 25% of the companies are owned by World China.

This means that around 35% of the local economy depends on them and they produce around **the 3.5 % of the Italian GDP (III),(and not mention to the privileged channel for Made in China than after they re-sell as Made in the EU. And this generates works not only in Veneto but in the whole Italy and revenues for the Italian as well as for the Local Governments).**

An interesting and positive example of integration.

Notes:

I) http://prosumerzen.wordpress.com/2011/01/25/spy-spy-oh-my-dear-spy-12-2/

II) http://prosumerzen.wordpress.com/2011/02/06/spy-spy-oh-my-dear-spy-22/

III) if you consider that the Transnational Organized Crime in Italy generates around the 10% of the GDP you can understand the interesting impact on the economy. **And this time with the World China we talk about LEGAL money!**

(Form of NSA:States within States)

Chap.58 -The Great X

Posted on February 23, 2011

There is a big misunderstanding when we tell that Gadhafi is menacing and killing his own people. Not at all he,(as well others in Libya), knows that he is not killing his own people. His own people is only his tribe. That is the point that we are missing a key point to understand the situation. If we look at his dress on his TV speech ,(22-2-11), he was dressed as the leader of his own tribe and most of what he calls as "supporters" are the members of this clan based in the region of Tripoli. He is not attacking his people,(his tribes), but other tribes that are ,(like in the KSA and not only),menacing his personal power and that of his Clan. To be clear "others" that he does not consider as his own people and this explains also why he used a crude and racist tone to describe them as "rats to kill".

Libya is another example of ethno-genesis ,(I), that means a "mix" of different people around a leading group due to some pressure. In this case ,when we face ethno-genesis (II), we have the each components lose some of its characteristic to mix and this "social mix" last till all have a common interest.

In this case to share the wealth generated by the natural resources of the land. And in this case the different peoples are the Clans.

This approach introduces to us the " Great X", what is that ?

The Great X is a new actor and we can call it as the Tribe, (Clan).

And in this phase it seems to be stronger than the religious variable, (and the related Umma),among the region. From Morocco to Bahrain the Clan plays a strategic role, (even in Syria where the current elite, the Assad family, has its stronghold among its tribe).

Different could be the situation in Morocco and Jordan where the ruling royal Families have a direct blood ties with the Holy Prophet Mohammed.

If the tribe is the key factor as it is we can better understand why today Gadhafi ordered to his Presidential Guard to sabotage the oil infrastructures. Why ?

He is pressing the other Tribes with the menace to destroy the resource of their wealth if they do not stop to revolt against him ,(III).

The Clan ,the Tribe is the new (almost unknown) variable ,(the Great X), we have to start to add inside the geo-political equation of the region.

Notes :

(I) Peter B. Golden ,An introduction of the history of the Turkic people : ethno-genesis and the formation in medieval and early modern Eurasia and Middle east. – 1992 Harrassowitz
Miklos Erdy , Hun and Xiongnu type Cauldron finds throughout Eurasia – 1995 Eurasian Studies Yearbook VI
Etienne de la Vaissiere , Huns et Xiongnu -2005 Central Asiatic Journal
(II) We do not consider ethno-genesis like the abused and degenerated meaning used by nazi ,neo-nazi and contemporary far right .See (I) to understand the correct meaning that hast **NOTHING to do** with racist implications.
(III) http://prosumerzen.wordpress.com/2011/02/21/tactical-warning-3-libya/

Books published by the Author with JEWIR.

Paolo Dealberti´s books are all cataloged by the Library of the Congress of the United States of America.

-Novels : (La Saga degli Speculari)

I.   Etnia Avatar

II. Obiettivo: Fermare Obama

To be puslished:

III. Humanpolitics

IV. Grecia: debito 2.0

V. Utopia Reale

-International Politics and Economy:

I.   Governi Pubblici Vs. Governi Non Statali. La vera guerra che attraversa il mondo

II. Legittimacy

III. State Actors Vs. Not State Actors

To be published:

IV. Italia Responsabilita´1.0

V. Ak47: Noi Vs Noi,(vincere contro il terrorismo e perdere contro il terrore)

VI. Zenprosumer, lifestyle 2.0

You can follow Paolo Dealberti at:

www.appealpower.com

www.ingramcontent.com/pod-product-compliance
Lightning Source LLC
Chambersburg PA
CBHW070859290526
45795CB00001B/179